LISTEN, YANKEE

BOOKS BY C. WRIGHT MILLS

LISTEN, YANKEE
  The Revolution in Cuba
IMAGES OF MAN *(1960)*
  (Edited with an Introduction)
THE SOCIOLOGICAL IMAGINATION *(1959)*
THE CAUSES OF WORLD WAR THREE *(1958)*
THE POWER ELITE *(1956)*
CHARACTER AND SOCIAL STRUCTURE *(1953)*
  (with H. Gerth)
WHITE COLLAR *(1951)*
THE PUERTO RICAN JOURNEY *(1950)*
  (with C. Senior and R. Goldsen)
THE NEW MEN OF POWER *(1948)*
FROM MAX WEBER: *Essays in Sociology (1946)*
  (Ed. and Tr. with H. Gerth)

LISTEN, YANKEE

The Revolution in Cuba

C. Wright Mills

McGRAW-HILL BOOK COMPANY, INC.
New York   Toronto   London

LISTEN, YANKEE

CONTENTS

Note to the Reader   7

ONE: What Does Cuba Mean?   13

TWO: Our Revolution   37

THREE: Your Counterrevolution   54

FOUR: Do-It-Yourself Economics   71

FIVE: Communism and Cuba   91

SIX: Revolutionary Euphoria   113

SEVEN: Culture in Cuba   133

EIGHT: What Does "Yankee" Mean?   151

Notes and Acknowledgments   190

NOTE TO THE READER, I

This book reflects the mood as well as the contents of discussions and interviews with rebel soldiers and intellectuals, officials, journalists and professors in Cuba during August, 1960. But it is about more than Cuba. For Cuba's voice today is a voice of the hungry-nation bloc, and the Cuban revolutionary is now speaking— most effectively—in the name of that bloc. What the Cubans are saying and doing today, other hungry peoples in Latin America are going to be saying and doing tomorrow. That prospect is neither Cuban boast nor Cuban threat. It is a distinct probability. In Africa, in Asia, as well as in Latin America, the people behind this voice are becoming strong in a kind of fury they've never known before. As nations, they are young: to them the world is new.

In Cuba, the people of a hungry nation are in full revolutionary cry. Their entire history has been involved—in extremist ways—with the history of the United States; and their island is very close to the domain of the United States.

No matter what you may think of it, no matter what I think of it—Cuba's voice is a voice that must be heard in the United States of America. Yet it has not been heard. It must now be heard because the United States is too powerful, its responsibilities to the world and to itself are too great, for its people not to be able to listen to every voice of the hungry world.

If we do not listen to them, if we do not hear them well, we face all the perils of ignorance—and with these, the perils of disastrous mistakes. If we do not listen, let us realize that other powerful nations are listening— certainly the Russians. They are hearing well the voices of the hungry world—and they are acting. Some of the mistakes of ignorance have already been made, in our

7

name, by the United States Government—and with disastrous consequences everywhere in the world for the
image and for the future of the United States. But perhaps it is not too late for us to listen—and to act.

I

My major aim in this book is to present the voice of
the Cuban revolutionary, as clearly and as emphatically
as I can, and I have taken up this aim because of its
absurd absence from the news of Cuba available in the
United States today. You will not find here The Whole
Truth About Cuba, nor "an objective appraisal of the
Cuban revolution." I do not believe it is possible for anyone to carry out such an appraisal today, nor do I believe that anyone—Cuban or North American—can yet
know "the whole truth about Cuba." That truth, whatever it turns out to be, is still being created, and every
week it changes. The true story of the Cuban revolution,
in all its meaning, will have to wait until some Cuban,
who has been part of it all, finds the universal voice of
his revolution.

In the meantime, my task has been to try to ask a few
of the fruitful questions, and then to seek out and to
listen well to as full a variety of answers as I could find.

The facts and the interpretations presented in these
letters from Cuba accurately reflect, I believe, the views
of the Cuban revolutionary. Most of the words are mine
—although not all of them; the arguments, the tone, the
interpretations, the tang and feel—they are in the main
directly Cuban. I have merely organized them—in the
most direct and immediate fashion of which I am capable.
Here, I am trying to say, is what Cubans in the middle
of their revolution are now thinking about that revolution, about its place within their own lives, and about its
future. Here is something of their optimism, their exhaus-
tion, their confusion, their anger, their ranting, their
worries—and yet, if you listen well, you will catch the
reasonable tone which does pervade the revolutionary
argument when it is discussed seriously and in private.

This revolution in Cuba is an enormous popular thrust.

The voice of Cuba today is the voice of revolutionary euphoria. It is also an angry voice. I am trying to express something of all this along with the Cubans' reasons for it. For their reasons are not only theirs: they are the reasons of all the hungry world.

II

Until the summer of 1960, I had never been in Cuba, nor even thought about it much. In fact, the previous fall, when I was in Brazil, and in the spring of 1960, when I was in Mexico for several months, I was embarrassed not to have any firm attitude towards the Cuban revolution. For in both Rio de Janeiro and Mexico City, Cuba was of course a major topic of discussion. But I did not know what was happening there, much less what I might think about it, and I was then busy with other studies.

In the late spring of 1960, when I decided "to look into Cuba," I first read everything I could find and summarized it: partly as information and partly in the form of questions to which I could find no answers in print. With these questions, and a few ideas on how to go about getting answers to them, I went to Cuba.

That journey has forced me to the view—a view which for a long time I had rejected—that much of whatever you have read recently about Cuba in the U.S. press is far removed from the realities and the meaning of what is going on in Cuba today.

I am not altogether clear as to how to explain this fact; I do not think it is simple. Unlike many Cubans, I do not believe that it is entirely due to a deliberate campaign of vilification. Yet it is true that if U.S. businesses adversely affected by the revolution do not coordinate your news of Cuba, business as a system of interests (which includes the media of mass communication) may nonetheless be a controlling factor in what you are able to know about Cuba today.

It is also true that the news editor's demand for violent headlines does restrict and shape the copy journalists produce. Editors and journalists tend to feel that the United States public would rather read about executions than about new lands put into cultivation. They print what they think is the salable commodity.

Our ignorance of Cuba is also, in part, due to the fact that the revolutionary Government of Cuba does not yet have a serviceable information agency for foreign journalists. In Cuba today it is not easy to get firm facts, and it is impossible to understand what is going on without skilled help from the people who are themselves in the middle of their revolution. In many cases such people are quite unable to help, if only because they are so busy carrying out the revolution. But it is more than that: they are increasingly unwilling to help, for they feel that their trust has been betrayed. Due to what they rightly consider sad experiences, they have come to feel that North American journalists will not recognize, or will distort, the truth, even when they see it before them.

I believe another source of trouble is that many North American journalists simply do not know how to understand and to report a revolution. If it is a real revolution—and Cuba's is certainly that—to report it involves much more than the ordinary journalist's routine. It requires that the journalist abandon many of the clichés and habits which now make up his very craft. It certainly requires that he know something in detail about the great variety of left-wing thought and action in the world today. And most North American journalists know very little of that variety. To most of them, judging from our newspapers, it all appears as just so much "communism." Even those with the best will to understand, by their very training as well as the restraints upon their work, are not able to report fully enough and accurately enough the necessary contexts, and so the meanings, of revolutionary events. In all truth, I do not know that anyone has all the necessary capacities; it is an extraordinarily difficult task for any member of an overdeveloped society to report what is going on in the hungry world today.

But one thing is clear: We are not getting in the United States sound information about it. Perhaps the truth is this: The mass media of information are often less coordinated by advertising pressures, official handouts, and off-the-record talks than by the ignorance and

confusion in the minds of those who are running them.
In brief: it is probable that some newspapers are often
coordinated; it is certain that many newsmen—like all
men—are often self-deceiving.

III

Having said that, I must immediately add that whatever may be truthful or useful in this book is due less to
any skill on my part as a social investigator than to my
good fortune in having been given complete access to information and experience by Cubans close to events who,
once trust is established, are eager to tell everything they
know and to express everything they feel. That trust was
given to me not because of any viewpoint I held towards
them or towards their revolution but simply because of
their acquaintance with previous books of mine.

My sources include discussions with most of the
leaders of the revolutionary Government of Cuba. I spent
three and a half 18-hour days with Prime Minister Fidel
Castro, and five or six days with René C. Vallejo, Head
of INRA, (*Instituto Nacional de Reforma Agraria*) in
the province of Oriente. I wish to thank them for the
generosity and patience with which they tolerated my
many questions in the middle of their long days and
nights of work.

I am also most grateful for the time they gave me to
Osvaldo Dorticos Torrado, the President of the Republic
of Cuba; Enrique Oltuski, former Minister of Communi-
cations, and now Director of Organization of the Industrialization Department of INRA; Ché Guevara, President
of the National Bank of Cuba; Raul Cepero Bonilla,
Minister of Commerce; Armondo Hart, Minister of Education; Carlos Franqui, Editor-in-Chief of *Revolución;*
Franz Stettmeier of the University of Oriente; Elvira
Escobar of the same institution; Margery Rios, and her
assistants of the Foreign Ministry; Isabel Rielo of the
first School City in the Sierra Maestra; Captain Escalona,
Aide to the Prime Minister; Elba Luisa Batista Benitez and
Lauro Fiallo Barrero of Manzanillo; Saul Landau, U.S.A.,
who shared with me the results of his own astute experi-

ence of Cuba; Robert Taber, U.S.A., who facilitated my trip to Cuba and my work while there. Lastly, I should like to thank Juan Arcocha, Deputy to Carlos Franqui, who interpreted for me in many long interviews and during much hard travel, and more than that, helped me to understand many things in Cuba.

Specific names are not cited in the text: for convenience of presentation and for brevity I have on given topics combined my discussions with different people; many passages are, in fact, "composite interviews." In addition, having been given the privilege of seeing whatever I asked to see and candid answers to all the questions I asked, I do not feel direct quotation is permissible.

IV

It is possible to entertain about Cuba several nightmare hypotheses. But if these nightmares are to be overcome, if they are to be made the bases of fruitful worry and of constructive policies towards Cuba, surely it is first of all necessary to know what the argument, the hopes, and the problems of the Cuban revolutionaries are. It is my task to state some of these.

That is why, in writing this book, I have thought the expression of my own views much less important than the statement of the Cuban revolutionaries' case. And that is why, insofar as I have been able, I have refrained from expressing a personal opinion. I have tried hard not to allow my own worries for Cuba, or for the United States, to intrude upon this presentation of the Cuban voice, nor have I attempted either to conceal or to underline such ambiguities as I happen to find in their argument.

Please know, then, as you read these letters, that it is the Cuban revolutionaries who are talking to you. After you have listened to them, I shall make a brief comment of my own.

C. WRIGHT MILLS

September 1960
Columbia University
New York City

ONE

WHAT DOES CUBA MEAN?

We Cubans know that you believe we are all led by a bunch of Communists, that the Russians are soon going to set up a rocket base, or something like that, here in Cuba, aimed at you; that we have killed thousands of people—out of hand—and are still doing it; that we have no democracy or freedom; and that we have no respect for private property.

What you believe about us, after all, is your business: we don't really care. Anyway, much of what you believe —true or false—doesn't matter as much to us as it does to you. But we, too, have beliefs—and fears. We fear you may be growing very impatient, and so thinking: "Shouldn't we just go down there and take over those troublemakers? We've helped them plenty, and instead of thanks they've turned against us, and now they've brought communism to our very door. Let's stop fooling around, and put an end to that Cuban mess."

It is because we know you are thinking such things that we are writing these letters to you. Or—if you'll forgive us—we write to you because we believe that you have lost touch with us.

As human beings, it is true, we Cubans have never had any close relations with you. But as peoples, each with its own government, now we are so far apart that there are Two Cubas—ours, and the one you picture to yourselves. And Two North Americas, too—yours, whatever it be, and the one we think about among ourselves.

Perhaps this would not matter so much were it not that we know our Cuba has become a new beginning in the Western Hemisphere, and maybe even in the world. It could be a new beginning for you, too, we suppose. But however all that may turn out, there's no doubt about one thing: It's a new beginning among us.

13

To most of us—and we want you to know this above all else—our new beginning is the very best thing that has ever happened to us. To some of us—and we suppose to most of you—much of it is uncertain, obscure, bewildering. But aren't new beginnings always like that? We Cubans are traveling a road no people of the Americas has ever traveled before. We don't know, we can't know, exactly where it leads. But we do fear that what you do and what you fail to do might well affect the question. For that's how it is in the world today, and that's especially how it is between Yankees and Cubans. And that does worry us; for you see, it's *our* destiny, and now we simply do not understand you, if we ever did.

Your Government will no longer talk with us—at least not to make any sense to us; so we are writing to you directly. We are trying to say that we are not some distant "question" about some far-off "international politics." We are not—as you might think—"another comic opera those crazy Latins are up to." To us the question of Cuba is first of all the question of how we are going to live—or even for how long. And you are involved in this, so we are trying to get into touch with you.

Like everyone else in the world, we believe it is good for men to understand each other, and we don't think that you do understand who we are, how we got this way, what we are now trying to do, and what the obstacles along our road may be. And, as we've just said, we don't understand you either. So we are writing to you.

I

And we are not angry with you, whoever you are; we don't even know you. How could we? The North America we know is not the suburbs of Cincinnati, wherever that is; how could we know anything about that? What we know is the big, sharp edges of Yankee politics and Yankee imperialism. To us, those are not just dirty words. They've been facts of our everyday lives as we've lived them in Cuba. It's been the idle tourists and the sugar monopolies and the support of the Batista dictatorship and the giving of medals to his murderers and our not having work to do and seeing the land lie idle while we squatted on the edge of the road in our filthy huts—that is what most of us know of North America.

But we're getting ahead of ourselves. There's so much to tell you and so little time. Let us first ask what do you really know about us Cubans, anyway? And how did you find it out? Whatever you may think of us—how can you be sure of it? Consider for a moment how it's been that we've known each other.

Some of you came down to Havana—tens of thousands of you, in fact, during the fifties. Some of you came down just to lie in the sun or on the beaches we Cubans were not allowed to use. But some of you came down to gamble and to whore. We stood on our street corners and watched you in your holiday place in the sun, away from your bleak, Yankee winter. Some of us have begged from you; we were hungry, you see. But know this: that's over; we are not going to do that sort of thing again, ever.

The gay tourist city of Havana—in the old days it was more than a place of sin. We Cubans, like everyone else, we know all about sin, being Catholics of a sort. But in Havana, sin was also the big money for the few, and every filthy practice of the brothel for girls 12 and 14 years old, fresh from their *bohios*. On the Prado and on the narrow street called The Street of Virtues, they and their pimps solicited you—and then Batista and his henchmen got their cut.

Maybe you don't know two facts about the gambling and the whoring. A lot of that gambling money ended up in the pockets of a corrupt Cuban Government, which your Government and some of your corporations supported and helped. Also much of it ended up in the pockets of your gangsters from Chicago and New York and Los Angeles. The money you paid for our whoring sisters—much of that money, too, ended up in the pockets of those corrupted and corrupting touts of the Batistas. It was a whoredom run by gangsters.

Nobody knows how many of our sisters were whores in Cuba during the last years of the Batista tyranny. In Havana, two years before the downfall of the tyranny, there were some 270 overcrowded brothels, there were dozens of hotels and motels renting rooms by the hour, and there were over 700 bars congested with *meseras*— or "hostesses"—the first step towards prostitution. There were about 12 *meseras* to each bar and they each earned from the bar about $2.25 a day. The employer and the Government grafter each got about $52 a day out of it. As for the gambling, it was not convenient for anyone to keep records, but slot machines in the tens of thousands were everywhere on the island. It was a thorough and complete racket, controlled, directly or indirectly, by the big men of the tyranny.

That old Havana, as we've said, was one of your holiday places, away from your bleak winter. But it was not away from your almighty dollar; it was not away from your perversions of leisure. Whatever Cuba has been in all these respects, you helped make it that: by your support of "our" Government, by your gangsters who were in on it, and by the patronage and the whims of your rich tourists. Well, that's over, Yankee. Please know that: We've drawn a line and we're standing on it. We've made laws and we're sticking to them, with guns in our hands. Our sisters are not going to be whores for Yankees any more.

So, anyway, you knew us as tourists know people, and that's not knowing very much.

II

For the rest, how have you known about us? By what your newspapers and magazines have said of us. And about this, we Cubans are very sure of one fact: most of your newspapers and magazines have lied to you, and they are lying to you now. Some of these lies are not really deliberate, although they do put false pictures of us into your mind. They are based on ignorance or carelessness or the laziness of many of your journalists. But not all the lies are like that: some of them are as deliberate as they can be, and we think you ought to know why. We think at least some of your newspapers must be owned or otherwise related closely to Yankee economic interests that have been hurt by our revolution.

In Cuba we understand about such things very well. That's the way it was in our old order in Cuba. There was much outright censorship, too, many pay-offs to the press, and "presidential decrees," and frequent "suspensions of constitutional guarantees" for one part of the country or for the whole of it. All that, too, was part of the reason why you haven't known us well. It was our own press as well as yours.

But yours is still going at it. Yours is still keeping us apart.

Everyone in the world who isn't limited to *Time* Magazine and the Hearst papers, and listening to your networks and all the rest of it, is getting to know something of the truth about Cuba today. They're getting to know that your press on Cuba is about as real as your quiz programs have been. They are both full of outrageous lies which may fool Yankees but don't fool anyone else. They are frauds, and other people are beginning to realize it, even if you do not.

The weaker and the more dependent—don't they have sharper eyes? Don't they use their brains more? Maybe we don't see it all straight, maybe we don't reason about it well, but now we are seeing and we are reasoning. And some things have not been hard to see.

When we triumphed in January 1959, *Life* described our Prime Minister, Fidel, as "the soldier-scholar" who had brought down Batista's "oppressive, corrupt and commercially astute" regime. But in seven months they were writing: "What was the glory and noble purpose in January has turned into demagoguery and chaos in July."

Well, it's more than a year now since then: What "chaos"? And as for "demagoguery"—if what Fidel teaches us is that, let us have more of it!

All your newspapers have kept predicting chaos and disaster for us. But here we are, Yankee, firm as a rock in the Caribbean, and moving on; our revolution is moving on.

Anyway, read the British newspapers—they've been much more honest about us than yours.

And doesn't everyone, even in North America, know by now what your own Herbert Matthews has said? "In my 30 years on the New York *Times,*" he said, "I have never seen a big story so misunderstood, so badly handled, and so misinterpreted as the Cuban revolution." That's no Cuban propagandist talking to you; that's one of your own best men, addressing your own American Society of Newspaper Editors on 21 April, 1960. For some reason which we don't understand, Mr. Matthews doesn't write about Cuba any more. Maybe somebody up there stopped him; or maybe he's gotten confused about our revolution as it's gone on, and, being an honest man, stopped writing. Anyway, a salute to Herbert Matthews for what he wrote about us during our insurrection.

We know newspapers often lie, and never tell the whole truth. We hope that you're not fooled. Anyway, we're not. We're too close up to what they are writing about us. Besides, as revolutionaries, we don't believe anything that we don't know personally: that's one thing making a revolution teaches you. Revolution is a way of defining realities.

We suppose that off and on you've been hearing about Latin America since you were in high school, and we can imagine how boring it must have been for you. What you've heard, mainly, is about how one dictator has replaced another, and about bits and pieces of ancient history, and then those crowds rioting in the sultry streets. You haven't paid much attention to it, except to the violence now and then; and we can hardly blame you for it. But you can't afford to ignore us any longer.

For now our history is part of your present.

And now some of the American future is ours, too, as well as yours.

What is happening in Cuba today is not boring; it is not just another episode; it is not merely, as you might think, local stuff; it is not just another palace revolution; it is not something way off somewhere else. And you cannot understand it without understanding the history it is coming out of.

III

You say, or you think, "We haven't done anything to you Cubans." Well, that is just not true: look at the history of our two countries, how they've been involved with each other. The facts are plain enough. We got most of them from North American books, as well as out of our own misery in Cuba.

First, in 1848, you tried to buy Cuba outright, for $100 million. You tried again a few years later. Do you realize what that means? But Spain would not sell, and the U.S. was not satisfied. The Old South wanted Cuba for slavery. And when they couldn't buy it, some U.S. envoys issued the "Ostend Manifesto." Cuba, it said, was geographically part of the United States; if the United States could not buy it, "by every law, human and divine, the United States had the right to take it by force." Your Southerners, in brief, wanted to turn Cuba into *two* slave states!

But that was a long time ago, and it didn't come off, this remarkable "Manifesto." Yet again in 1861 your Southern slave owners looked "forward to the time when Cuba" as well as "Central America and Mexico" would "fall into Southern hands" and be occupied by slave owners.

It didn't come off; Cuba remained under the Spanish yoke; and against that yoke we Cubans continued to revolt. In the late 1860's we began an uprising that lasted for the next ten years; we demanded that the slaves be freed and that Cubans govern their own island. But still the slaves were not freed—until 20 years later—and Cuba was not independent.

Then, finally, it began to happen. In 1895, inspired by José Martí, we made an insurrection and tens of thousands of soldiers sent from Spain couldn't cope with our guerrillas. The next year, the Spanish sent a big general—Valeriano Weyler, that was his name, and he was a butcher. He "turned Cuba into a series of concentration camps," and in them we suffered; whole sections of our civilian population were herded into them, and we suffered.

But also many Spanish soldiers died. True, for a long time Cubans failed; true, our countryside was laid waste; true, out of our misery Yankee businessmen made money. They bought land cheap after the devastation of our wars with Spain. During the last twenty years of the 19th century Yankee bankers went all out for sugar plantations. By 1896 they had about $30,000,000 of our property, even back then. Also, they bought up Cuban mines—iron, nickel, manganese. Bethlehem Steel and the Rockefeller interests—they began to buy us up. By the time this century began, the Yankees owned $50 million worth of Cuban sugar land, and tobacco, and mines. You were pretty busy back then going west, but some of you were already busy going south, too.

Meanwhile, what were we Cubans doing?

Working, as usual, when we could get the work.

But also fighting Spain for our independence, and dying for that. The rest of Latin America, most of it, had already thrown off the old Spanish yoke, decades before, but Cubans were still chafing against it at the turn of the 20th century.

And then came—the Yankee Marines. Our revolutions in Cuba—first against Spain, then against the Yankees—they've come closer together than in most of Latin America. We are the last of the 19th-century revolutions and, maybe, the first of the 20th-century ones unless you count Mexico. But back to the history for a moment. As we Latin Americans often say: "After the Yankee dollar, the Yankee flag." At first we thought you were going to help us to be really free, but it didn't turn out that way. In 1901, the U.S. forced upon Cuba something called the Platt Amendment. This Platt Amendment simply took away our sovereignty. Whenever your Government pleased, it could meddle into Cuban affairs, and also it restricted what the Cuban Government could do and could not do. It gave Yankees the right (what a word that is, the way your State Department and monopolies use it), "the right" to come into Cuba with guns in their hands if they wished, to intervene to see to it that the Government here was protecting Yankee property. And that's just what they did.

The first time was before the Platt Amendment, in

1899: one of your generals and his troops occupied our island—after we had just about whipped the Spanish who had been occupying us before you. The Yankee soldiers left in 1902, leaving behind the right to have a naval base—for $2,000 a year!—at our Guantánamo Bay; as we write to you in August 1960 the base is still here.

But you did it again and again: Yankee troops came in 1906. Again in 1912. Again in 1917. And in 1920 you controlled our Government directly, without even using your own troops.

In the meantime, as we say in Latin America, "The Yankee dollar was following the Yankee flag."

Violence and cash, cash and violence—is that all Yankees think about? Is that your only way of solving problems and *dealing*—it's a good Yankee word—of dealing with people?

But forgive us, perhaps it's not you. But it *is* your State Department and your sugar corporations and your Pentagon. We Cubans know this—abstractly; some of us still believe it, and so we still believe in you, whoever you are—abstractly.

But friend, you really should do something about these people. It *is* your Government, isn't it? All this is your business. And you've got to attend to it now. Or you are going to wreck us all.

Of course, we Cubans do realize that all this sort of Yankee intervention wasn't going on only in Cuba. It was happening all around the world, but especially all around Latin America. One of your own generals—Smedley D. Butler—remembered it in the middle thirties, and wrote in one of your magazines:

"I spent thirty-three years and four months in active service as a member of our country's most agile military force—the Marine Corps. I served in all commissioned ranks from a second lieutenant to major general . . . I helped make Mexico and especially Tampico safe for American oil interests in 1914. I helped make Haiti and Cuba a decent place for the National City Bank boys to collect revenues in . . . I helped purify Nicaragua for the international banking house of Brown Brothers in 1909–1912. I brought light to the Dominican Republic for

American sugar interests in 1916. I helped make Honduras 'right' for American fruit companies in 1903. In China in 1927 I helped see to it that Standard Oil went its way unmolested.

"During those years I had, as the boys in the back room would say, a swell racket. I was rewarded with honors, medals, promotions. Looking back on it, I feel I might have given Al Capone a few hints. The best *he* could do was to operate his racket in three city districts. We Marines operated on three *continents*."

That was no Cuban revolutionary talking to you; that was not our Fidel Castro "ranting again"; that was one of your own men, a general at that, telling you what it was all about—Major General Smedley D. Butler of the U.S. Marine Corps.

But let's get back to Cuba. As we were saying, the dollar and the flag, they were all mixed up together. In the late nineties only 10 percent of our sugar production came through mills owned by Yankees. Just before the First World War, about one-third. By the middle twenties, the figure was two-thirds.

Corrupted Cuban politicians and your absentee capitalists, they got together, and they did back in the twenties what your historians call "The Dance of the Millions."

Our politicians were grafters and lackeys; your capitalists were upright, honorable men in New York, who paid off the grafters and took out the big money. And we Cubans? We were the vassals of both. It wasn't what *we* did or what *we* didn't do that was making our history and our way of life what it was. It was what was decided in the Directors' Rooms on lower Manhattan.

And we didn't even know those men.

We never saw any of them.

IV

Well, all of that was a few decades ago, after all— we suppose it's best for us all to try to forget it. It's for our fathers to remember. What we remember was yesterday and the day before. But for us, well, we think until the revolution our days were pretty much the same as the days of our fathers. In many ways they were worse, if only because we knew more about the world than our fathers knew.

Your Government said it was protecting and guaranteeing our Cuban independence but that independence was a sham. It was your Government and your corporations that decided when our "independence" was menaced and so when the Yankees could intervene. What they had was the key to our house.

Before our revolution—in 1956—those men in the Directors' Rooms on lower Manhattan controlled more than 90 percent of our electricity and telephones, about half of what was called our "public service" railroads; some 40 percent of our sugar production.

And the Cuban Government? Well, your Government and corporations had much to do with that and at times ran it outright. No one who knows the score, certainly none of your own Yankee historians and scholars, denies that those who ruled us were mainly incompetent despots, venal grafters—and often, especially towards the end, bloody butchers.

Fulgencio Batista seized the power of the army in 1933, and with it he seized the Government of Cuba. Your Government "recognized" him as the true Government of Cuba almost immediately. The Yankees didn't intervene then, you can be sure, and he ruled over us, with the power of the army, for ten years. Then again, in 1952, after the war for the Four Freedoms was all over and done with, Batista came back into power, again by getting hold of the army and using it to take over, and again your Government said: "OK, Señor Batista, you're our boy." Very soon then his blood bath began. Before we threw Batista out, late in 1958, this butcher and his gangsters, trained by your Military Missions, using guns and planes and tanks your Government gave to him, had murdered some 20,000 Cubans.

To Batista, anyone who was against him, anyone who complained out loud about anything, was A Dirty Communist. And always his answer was the same: torture

them, mutilate them, kill them all. He was no sentimen-
talist, Batista; he was a sick barbarian, a cruel savage
with lethal weapons and modern torture at his command.
In Havana alone, God only knows how many men and
boys were castrated; and when women were raped, their
husbands were made to look upon it. Batista's police
stations were torture chambers; his bully boys were
everywhere, kicking, stealing, arresting, smashing. And
always the same excuse: "The Dirty Communists, they
are trying to take over our fine little democracy."

While all this was going on, in the 1950's—just yesterday, it seems to us—for four and a half years, the
Eisenhower government sold bombs and war planes and
bullets and guns to this gangster and dictator. They always said it was for Hemispheric Defense. But what is
the truth? Those weapons were certainly not used for
any such thing as hemispheric defense. They were used
to kill Cubans. And that's one reason that whenever we
Cubans hear talk about "hemispheric defense," we shud-
der.

Batista had a big mansion at Daytona Beach, Florida.
He was cheered as a great and noble man of the noble
"free world"—outside Cuba. In his rooms, in glass
cases, he kept his medals of honor, received from the
Yankee Government and from other allied powers. The
ones he'd gotten earlier—from Hitler and Mussolini—he
had burned up or thrown away.

Your ambassadors—hear their names, Yankee, and
send them to disgrace!—Mr. Arthur Gardner and Mr.
Earl E. T. Smith—they ate and drank with the Batista
dictator. Did they tell you what was going on? Did they
tell you about the inhuman outrages, or did they just
watch the sugar quotations? Did your radios, your newspapers, all your TVs, did they tell you all about how
bombs made in the U.S.A. were the bombs used to kill
thousands of Cubans in the city of Cienfuegos in September of 1957? Did they tell you that shortly after those
bombings, the United States Air Force decorated the
Cuban general of Batista who directed those air attacks?
Did they tell you *that*, on the front pages, in the big
print, in all the newspapers? And if they did, Yankee,
what did you do about it? If they did tell you, what did

you do—about the weapons, for example, the Yankee Government kept sending—and sending—and sending—to Batista?

We Cubans, how can we help but wonder what kind of a people you are? Can't you understand why we shout so, now that we are able at last to shout what we really feel, what we really know, what we've suffered.

If we Cubans have "gone to extremes," know this: so have you Yankees. We've been involved with each other in *extremist* ways. The abuses printed in Cuba against the Yankees have been well overbalanced by the abuses printed in the United States against us Cubans. On both sides, some of these statements are extreme, maybe even absurd—for anybody can get carried away, and in every fight many always do.

But much that we've said against you is simply the plain, miserable truth, and we know it is because we have lived it; and you don't know it because you have not lived it.

Our country, our Cuba, it *was* simply a political colony of the United States at least until F.D.R., and even after that.

Our Cuba, our country, it *was* simply an economic colony of the U.S. monopolies until our revolution.

And all the time, Cuba was a place of misery and filth, illiteracy and exploitation and sloth—a caricature of a place for human habitation. And it is out of all that, the Cuban revolution is struggling. Keep that big fact in mind, Yankee; write it into your conscience when you read about what's happening in Cuba today. If you don't, as you might say, you can't get to first base in understanding what's going on.

We Cubans have had a highly visible standard of living —and of starving and dying, too—but you didn't see that, or if you did you just didn't care. We did, some of us. And all of us felt its meaning in our bellies. And now maybe you begin to see the results of some of us caring to the point of risking our lives to do something about it. You didn't do anything about it, you see. And that's what our revolution is all about. Our revolution is not about your fight with Russia, or about communism, or hemispheric defense, or any of that: all those words came later, partly forced down our throat by your Government and your monopolies.

Point number one, Yankee, is that our revolution is about our old Cuban standard of starving and our new Cuban standard of living. Of course, it's about more than that, much more. We are building, at breakneck speed, an entirely new society, and we did not inherit much to build it with from the old order in Cuba. From that we inherited disorder and grief. We're in a fluid moment and everything's at stake; like the men in the Sierra Maestra, now a whole nation of Cubans, we're camping out.

What's happening here, many of us believe, is one kind of solution for the peoples of the hungry nations that make up the continent to your south—for the peoples of this enormous continent and of its island fringes. Cuba today is coming to represent and to be understood as representing—a way out.

A way out of what?

The answer is just our point: a way out of the old order—in Cuba certainly, and maybe also everywhere in our part of America. That old order is an order of police terror and grief and poverty and disease and illiteracy and the corrupted politics of the thief and the capitalism of the robber—all of it of a sort you probably have never known. And it is out of that, that we think Cuba has taken a real way.

We know that you might be saying, "We haven't done anything to you Cubans." We know you feel that. And that's just the point: *You* haven't done anything.

We have to be honest with you, so we say: "We think you just don't care." Oh, we don't mean that you should care about us—we'll take care of ourselves now. We mean you don't care about what is being done by some Yankees in your name, and what is not being done by them. It makes us wonder about your kind of democracy. You can understand that, can't you?

Like you, only more so, we're a rhetorical people; we too love all the big words of our heritage, all those aspirations we used to think were shared by all the Western peoples, but which, these days, we think you seem all too often to forget, and some Yankees never even knew.

But listen, Yankee: we've come to a time when words are not enough. We've got to eat. We've got to use words to get rice and beans. We've got to remake the way we live so we can count on eating—all the year around, we mean, and not just when your sugar corporations give us work And we've got to defend ourselves, because we do believe that if we don't, your Government is going to try to crush us.

When you're in the middle of action and everything's at stake, you test what men say by what they do. We can't throw away words celebrating what we've already got. We've not got enough and we're in action and everything's at stake. We've got to use words to help our action. We're in a great storm on a big ocean crossing and we've got no time for playing around with your big words. Not just yet. Maybe that will come later. We are hopeful. But now we've got to use our own words to get our own beans and shoes, rice and tankers, chickens to eat and schools to go to, and also—it seems to us—also guns.

V

If you can understand the things we are now going to tell you, we think you'll be able to make up your own mind about what is going on in Cuba and what it might mean for you, as well as for us.

First of all, we Cubans are part of Latin America—not of North America. We speak Spanish, we are mainly rural, and we are poor. Our history is not like your history; it is part of Latin American history. And Latin America is 180,000,000 people, growing faster than you are growing, and scattered over a territory more than twice as large as the U.S.A.

Like much of Latin America, but more so, we're fed up with what your corporations and what your governments do down here. They've dominated us long enough, we've said it to ourselves now. Your Government supported Batista right up to the last minute of his gangster regime. But now Cuba is not just another island in the Caribbean. The Caribbean is not a North American lake. All that—that's over.

For unlike most of Latin America, we Cubans have done something about all of this, about exploiters from your country in Cuba and about our own Cuban exploiters of Cubans too. We are now doing it, and we are going to keep on doing it. We're not just a bunch of bums from up in the hills of the Oriente, and we are not in some comic opera. We mean business, your kind of business first of all: economic business for us.

Your big business interests and your Government, they don't like what we've done and what we're doing. Probably they are going to keep on not liking it; they are going to hate it more and more. And we are *not* sorry for that—except if they keep on fooling you about it.

But—and this is a very important thing—we are not alone in all this. We are not just 6½ million people sitting on a little island looking up at your 180 million sitting on a big continent. Those bad old days are gone. But who is with us?

First of all, we think, we hope, that many of the 180 million peoples of Latin America are with us. They may not like some things we've done and some things we may have still to do; that's inevitable in any revolution. A revolution is not a very polite thing and it's never altogether clear just where it's going, just where it has to go. But in our economic contest with the Yankee corporations and the Yankee Government we think most of the people of Latin America are with us and against your monopolies and against your Government; and, if need be, against their own governments as well.

We've got others with us too. All over the world people, especially the young ones and the students, those who can read and who can talk and write and who are hungry enough to read well, they are beginning to react against your policies and the warrior establishments of your cold war and of your monopoly economy.

So this is who we Cubans are:

We're part of Latin America.

We're fed up with Yankee corporations and governments.

We've done something about it.
Your corporations and your Government don't like it.
We are not alone.

Today the revolution is going on in Cuba. Tomorrow
—not next year—it is going to be going on elsewhere.
A revolution like ours does not come about just because
anyone wants it—although it takes that, too. Revolutions
in our time, we Cubans believe, come out of misery, out
of conditions like those of the old Cuba. Where such
conditions continue and there's a mountain nearby,
there'll be revolutions. And in Latin America and elsewhere there are many such countries still today in the
old sloth. That is why this continent is going to become
the scene of convulsions you've never dreamed of. You
can't buy off revolutions with $500 million of aid. You
can only buy off some Latin American governments—
and for that, it's far too much money; they can be bought
much cheaper! To head off revolutions, once they are
under way, it would take much more—and much more
than just money. We're talking sense to you, Yankee;
listen to us, please. What will happen, for example, when
the people of all those South American countries realize
their enormous wealth, both the actual and what
could be, and yet find themselves poor? then looking
across to tiny Cuba, they see that Cubans are not poor?
What will happen then?
We peoples of Latin America, we're beginning to wonder about a lot of things that we've just taken for granted,
or never thought of at all.
We live in the same hemisphere as you—so we've always been told. But what does that mean today? Even
without jets, from New York City it's ten hours to Guatemala—the same to London; it's the same time from
New York to Lima as it is to Vienna—sixteen hours. And
it's only six hours to Mexico City, but eleven to Paris.
So what does the mere fact that we live in the Western
Hemisphere mean anyway?

We are all part of "Western Civilization"—so we've
always been told. But are we really? All of us? We Latin
Americans die at the average age of thirty-five; you live

until you're past sixty-five. Our illiterate, disease-ridden, hungry peasant masses in Bolivia and Haiti and Venezuela, and yesterday in Cuba—are they part of the same "Western Civilization" as you? If so, isn't it a curious kind of a civilization in which such things can go on?

As long as they do go on, perhaps we Latin Americans had better realize that the people of whom we are a part is not part of whatever civilization you North Americans belong to. Once and for all, let us get it straight: we belong with the peoples of the hungry nations. That they live in Africa and Asia as well as in Latin America—that makes no difference.

Hunger is hunger.

To die before you reach thirty-five in Central America while working for the fruit company is not so different from dying in South Africa while working in a diamond mine.

Disease is disease.

And not to be able to read is the same in any language: it is to be a people without history; it is to be only half a man. Almost half of us Latin Americans are such primitive creatures—we are illiterate. What does "the free world," what does the "Western Civilization" of the Yankees mean to us?

If you still think that we are members of the same Western civilization as you, and if you value that civilization—whatever it means to you—then perhaps you'd better find out what is going on within what you take to be its confines. Many of us know only the confines.

Here's another thing about the world today we Cubans at least are becoming very much aware of. The Communist nations—just yesterday, and many of them still today—they too belong to the hungry-nation bloc.

It is that fact above all others which we do share with them. And it is simply a fact. If you think all your catastrophes around the world are caused by a mere handful of conspirators stirring up trouble, think about the hungry-nation bloc, Yankee. It's a lot more important than the Communist bloc or the Capitalist bloc. It's a lot more important to us at least, and it's us and not the rich Yankees we're talking about now.

No matter what else these Communist peoples may be or may not be, one thing is becoming clear to us: as hungry people they are coming *out* of hunger. They are building societies in which there isn't any more of all *that*. But when we look at the hungry peoples who are still under Capitalism—or as you so curiously say, who are still "free"—we don't see that kind of development. What we see, Yankee, is: people—still—hungry.

So you may not like it, so you might not even know it, but there are three big facts you are going to be living with from now on:

First, Russia and the Sino-Soviet bloc is a solid fact of world history. It's not going to just fade away or fall to pieces.

Second, starting from very nearly nothing, they've built up over there, in only a generation or two, an economy and a society that we—like you—in many ways find puzzling. But perhaps unlike you, we also find it in many ways attractive. In our bellies, we mean. But we will tell you some things about this question of Communist influences in Cuba later on. We know it is important to you; it's important to us, too, and to the rest of the world as well. But most of us are not worried about it—certainly not the way most of you seem to be. So, for now, here's the third big fact:

They are with us and they are against the Yankee monopolies and the Yankee Government. No doubt it's in their own selfish interests, but we do need help, if only in dealing with you. If we don't get it, you'll try to continue to exploit us; and you'll try to crush all our new beginnings in Cuba. That's what we believe. Make no mistake about this: We are going to take the help we need from whoever will give it to us. We are going to take it on our own terms, insofar as we can, but we've got to have it or you'll try hard to starve us out. And you are 200 times richer than we, and God alone knows how much more powerful.

VI

That power and wealth, Yankee, that's why it seems so crazy to us when your Government says to us as it has been saying that our Cuban Government was following ". . . a pattern of relentless economic aggression . . . against the United States. . . ." Now, please do think about that a moment. Isn't it slightly ridiculous? We are about six million people, you are 180 million. Your economy, as we've just said, is approximately 200 times the size and the wealth of ours. We don't even yet grow our own food, much less make the tractors we need to help us to grow it. You spend more in a year for lipstick and things like that than all of us down here earn for a full year's work. Under such circumstances, now isn't it a little bit silly to talk of "Cuba's relentless economic aggression against the United States of America"?

Your Government also says to us that our "economic aggression" is "designed to destroy Cuba's traditional investment and trade relations with the free world."

That, we must tell you, is a true statement of our intentions. But do you know what those "traditional investment and trade relations with the free world" were? First of all, they were not so much relations with any "free world"—unless you are willing (as we are not) to identify "the free world" with your big corporations. For our economic relations were overwhelmingly with them and only with them. In fact, they weren't so much "our" economic relations at all. They were economic relations within and between Yankee corporations. Our part in them was mainly to do the work, and to provide from our island the natural resources they took away from us. And it's those monopolies that are getting hurt—although very little, at that—by our buying of oil and other things we need from the Soviet bloc, and our selling sugar to those countries. How in the world can that commercial trading be considered "economic aggression" against "the United States," or, as Yankee hypocrites say, against "hemispheric solidarity"?

What solidarity? How can our commerce be defined, as your Mr. Lodge did in the U.N. on 19 July 1960, as "alien domination"? We think your Mr. Lodge is either an economic idiot or else an aggressive front-man for big Yankee monopolies.

Will your election of a new President for 1961 help us? It doesn't seem possible. Your two candidates compete in their belligerency towards us and in their ignorance of us. So far as any real alternatives for us are concerned—and for you, too, presumably—we think your election is a big fraud. What are we to suppose when Mr. Nixon speaks openly about bringing us to our knees whenever he decides to, and Mr. Kennedy "takes the hard line," and calls us a "Communist satellite." What that really means is that we are no longer a Yankee satellite. We are an independent and sovereign nation, and nobody's satellite. All the Kennedys and Nixons can see in the world is an imagined military scene, and both see that with all the vision of the hysteric.

But we may as well face it: We've now been declared by both your parties to be An Enemy of yours—another one!—although we might have been a friend. But then, we know about your "campaign rhetoric," and so we haven't lost all hope.

VII

Anyway, all that kind of nonsense is coming to a bad end—outside the U.S.A. at least. We Cubans *are* doing our best to help show it up for what it is. Surely you must know that all over the world there's been building up the hatred of what your Government and your monopolies have been doing? Most of that hate has had no chance to get out as yet, much less to come to your indifferent attention. But some of it has, and a lot more of it will.

About two years ago—remember?—your Vice President tried to make a good-will tour of South America. In Uruguay, Argentina, Paraguay, and Bolivia, Mr. Nixon and his company were often jeered and the questions put to him in press conferences got sharper and sharper. In Lima, Peru, "a serious demonstration" occurred. Mr. Nixon (we quote from your New York

Times) "was spat upon and stoned by a howling mob."
Then on to Caracas, capital of oil-rich, poor-people Venezuela: The rocks thrown got as big as melons; Mr.
Nixon's limousine was attacked; the "angry mob" attempted to overturn it, or to drag the Vice President
out into the street. Its windows shattered, spit-bedecked,
the car "jumped the curb and escaped in the traffic."
Later that day, the Army of Venezuela broke up demonstrations "with bayonets and tear gas." Then Yankee Marines and paratroopers were dispatched to Caribbean
bases.

Sixteen months later, in October 1959, left-wing students in Buenos Aires bitterly protested Yankee assistance to Argentina's national universities; they forced a
suspension of the program in the schools of economics
and in engineering. And there have been many more
such incidents, some reported, others not.

Then in the spring and summer of 1960 the results
of what you are doing and what you're leaving undone
really began to show up—dramatically, violently, as a series of little catastrophes for Yankeedom abroad.

In Turkey, student riots led to a military junta; it
took over the state, which before was run by Commu-
nist-Container Menderes. He's gone now.

In South Korea, students knocked over the corrupt,
Yankee puppet regime of Syngman Rhee. He's gone
now.

On Taiwan, the eight million Taiwanese under the
heel of your American-imposed dictator, Chiang Kai-
shek, with his two million Chinese, grew increasingly
restive. He's still there.

On Okinawa—one of the Yankee military bases around
the world—the people got their first chance since World
War II ended to demonstrate against the Yankees; and
some students took that chance, snake-dancing and
chanting angrily, "Go home, go home," to your visiting
President. But don't worry—twelve thousand Yankee
troops easily handled the generally grateful crowd, and
the President got to the airport in a helicopter.

In Japan weeks of student rioting succeeded in reject-
ing your President's visit, jeopardized a new Yankee

treaty, and displaced the big-business pro-Yankee Prime Minister Kishi.

That's not the complete list, but maybe it will show you what we're trying to tell you.

But why are we blaming you for all this? Because of your power, first of all, as we've already said. With such power as you have, if you do *not* act, you *are* acting. Don't you see that? And *you* didn't act, Yankee. And because of that, now you are the main target of this trouble and of this hate. All those tens of millions of people, they didn't just happen to pick on Yankees. They had some reasons, maybe wrong reasons—some of them —but do you even know what their reasons were? Have you ever tried to find them out? Are you trying to answer them, to speak to their condition?

But you might now be saying to yourself: "Well, maybe so, but anyway that's all over now; it will all go away; and besides, all that's way over there in Asia."

That's being provincial, Yankee. You must know that —with all your airplanes and tourism.

But however that may be, you can't shrug Cuba off like that! It's less than a hundred miles from the Keys of Florida; and for over sixty years at least it has certainly been closely enough tied up with Yankee action and Yankee inaction.

Tomorrow the returns from what you do and what you fail to do, everywhere in the hungry-nation bloc, will be even more evident. But will they be obvious enough to distract you from the energetic pursuit of your private affairs? That's a real question for us Latin Americans. It's a question for all Americans in the Western Hemisphere.

It's also a question about world history—today and tomorrow—a world history of which we are all a part, whether we want to be or not. What they are saying in the hungry nations, in the slum countries of the world, is that the rich Yankees pay attention only to money and to violence. And if you don't have the money, then all you've got left is the violence. Well, isn't that so? In the meantime, you've surely begun to realize that things are not under the old easy control. Your country—and so you, too, if it is your country any more—is becoming the target of a world hate such as easygoing Yankees have never dreamed of.

But listen, Yankee:

Does it have to be that way? Isn't it up to you? Isn't at least some of it up to you? As you think about that, please remember this:

Because we have been poor, you must not believe we have lost our pride. You must not believe we have no dignity, no honor, no fight. Now we are assuring you as calmly as we are able that we do have these qualities. In future we will continue to reveal them to you—by our actions as well as our words. Either you will see this, or you won't see it. If you do, perhaps we can be friends again. If you don't, it will be a very bad time of troubles for us all.

Don't you see that events cry out? Don't you see that events demand that you think, feel, act? Now that is true all over the world. But now such demanding events are, in part, Cuban events. Do we Cubans take satisfaction in this? Yes, of course, we do; we'd be less than human if we didn't. We don't take satisfaction in the fact that we are the center of the cold war in the Caribbean. We don't like the cold war anywhere—who does? We don't want to be the western Hungary—who does? But we are glad, we have to be glad, that finally many things that must be done are now being done in Cuba.

So what can we say to you to make you understand?

Can we say: Become aware of our agonies and our aspirations? If you do it will help you to know what is happening in the world you are living in. Take Cuba as the case; in terms of it, re-think who you are, American.

What does Cuba mean?

It means another chance for you.

TWO

OUR REVOLUTION

I was in the revolution almost from the beginning, and I will tell you about it from the inside. Not long after Fidel landed in the Oriente, in 1956, coming from Mexico where he had been in training, I got a gun and I went to join Fidel and his men.

Where did I get my gun? From you, of course—at least I guess you paid for it. Maybe you didn't know that, but it's true. It happened like this. You paid taxes to your Government and your Government took your money and bought my gun and gave it to Batista—that bloody bastard—and Batista gave it to one of his murdering gangsters. But one night up an alley, in a little town you wouldn't know the name of, four of us jumped him. I killed him myself with my machete—it was a war, Yankee—and so I got my gun off him. Then I went to the Sierra, to Fidel, and fought with him against all the Batistas.

Now there was a woman living in a house outside Santiago de Cuba, in the Oriente. She was an educated woman in her forties. Her house was up the mountain a way, in between the Batista army and the rebel soldiers. During the day the Batista soldiers came there and during the night the rebels. Her house was in between, you see. But she wasn't in between. She was with us, she was a revolutionary. She came from Manzanillo, where many revolutionaries have come from. So she helped us. She carried guns to us and bullets scattered among the beans. But mainly she bought medicines in Santiago and brought them to her house and we got them there; and messages, too.

How did she get away with it? Well, now you see how the mind of the capitalist works. She had a very rich uncle and her father wasn't so badly off either. And the rebels had taken some cattle from her father, to eat the meat. The Batista soldiers knew that. They had it down on a little card in their secret police files, so they were just absolutely sure that she was against the revolution. You see how they thought? But this woman, she always said to us, "It's another thing to thank Fidel for—those cattle you boys ate, it's saving my life."

We used to talk with her at night, and she would tell us what was going on in the city and how the revolution had come to her. She was an educated woman and she tried to tell us everything she knew because she was a revolutionary.

She was in Havana when Batista took power in 1952. The younger people had forgotten about Batista in the thirties, but she remembered, and she felt *insulted* seeing how the people didn't remember and just accepted it, how they didn't remember the horrors of Batista.

She was in Santiago when Fidel and the 170 young men and the two girls attacked the Batista garrison in Moncada, in 1953. She wasn't really in it, then, but she and some other women helped those boys get out of the city. She just got filled up with sentiment for what she called "those poor lost boys." But we told her they weren't lost and they weren't boys. They were revolutionaries and they were men and they were going to win. They had already won—they had torn the mask off Batista by that raid. Their brothers were taken prisoner and then murdered, and now everybody could see it: Batista was just a murderer. It was the turning point.

And then, Fidel landed in 1956 and it really began. Everybody knew he had come and that he wasn't killed as the Batistas said. Then in that long time, every day somebody was killed and we asked, How many today? How many? There wasn't any one moment when we knew we had won; we always knew we were going to win. But the truth is we didn't expect it to come so soon.

|

We Cubans like to talk about how our revolution began. Where *did* it all begin?

"Up in the Sierra Maestra, of course, in the province

of the Oriente," some say. "Yes, of course," say others, "but also in the classrooms of the law school and the medical school at the big university in Havana." "I don't believe that," says someone else, "I think it began in the hearts of the hungry peasants, in their *bohíos,* in their miserable, rural slums." Then some very old man, he says: "Perhaps that is true, but did it not really begin back while we were still under the Spanish yoke and José Martí wrote and fought for seven years and many of us were killed, and then the Yankee Marines took us over?"

The truth is, nobody knows just where it began, but one thing is sure; off and on, we've been fighting a long time. And here's another thing that's true: It isn't over yet; it's still going on. And it's in view of this, that we'd like to tell you some things about our revolution.

The revolution was incubated at the university. Now, you have to realize that universities in Latin America are just not like North American universities. In Cuba, even in the old order, Havana University was a curious island of thwarted freedom in the sea of Batista stupidity and tyranny. The professors who ran it took orders neither from the politicians nor the police. You might think this strange, but it really isn't. The students in the old order were mainly sons and daughters and friends of the ruling groups, the rich groups, and their radicalism was seen as "a passing phase," something they were just going through. Also, these students, after they grew up, were going to be the government officials and politicians, as well as the doctors and lawyers.

Of course, even so, students were beaten up by the Batista police, and shot at. And during the last year of the tyranny, the university was just closed down. But before all that the university was the cradle of the revolutionary ideas. And it was only at the university that any more or less free "politics" went on, and perhaps because of that the politics made there were the politics of revolt and insurgency, of rebellion—the politics of the revolution. The students were politicos, noisy and angry. They made speeches and put out manifestos, and they took to the streets. And it was in this place, this half-free island in the middle of the Cuban misery, that, beginning in 1945, Fidel Castro—son of a rich man and a student of law—found his gift as an orator.

Even back then, some who knew him say he was fluent to the point of being overwhelming. But some of his fellow students didn't like him much because he was political, you see, and "decent," honest, middle-class people didn't mix in politics. That was for thieves. They thought Fidel Castro just wanted to use everybody, to get to be a class delegate, and then a delegate of the faculties, and then president of the student federation, and so use this as a springboard into the same old Cuban politics. Everybody can see now how wrong this judgment was, and many of these same people are helping Fidel now day and night.

Anyway, when he finished his course of study, Fidel practiced law. And then, in 1952, he ran for the congress. You see, he tried first to do it by elections and all that. But that was the year Batista seized the power again with the army, and with one blow smashed all the bourgeois democracy:

"You are finished," Batista said to the President. "I am the government."

In just 11 days, 11 days, your Government "recognized" Batista as the Government in Cuba.

But Fidel Castro—he did *not* recognize this gangster.

And *that* is how it really began:

A man said No! to a monster.

At first he sued in the courts about the election. He submitted a brief that showed the Batista gang had violated laws. Of course the brief was thrown out. And then he began to see it: The only real politics possible for honest men in the old Cuba was the politics of the gun, the politics of the guerrilla. The revolution was the only "politics" for an honest man. The very next year, 1953, on the 26th of July, Fidel led the raid on Moncada.

Where did this young man come from? Who was he? He was born on 13 August 1926, the son of a prosperous sugar and lumber man in the Oriente. So he knew those mountains as a boy, hunting in them, and also seeing the poverty there. He went to Catholic schools, first in Santiago de Cuba—the big town in the Oriente—and then to a Jesuit high school in Havana and then Havana University, where he became a lawyer. In 1950, he had a busy law practice in Havana, but he was not like other lawyers; he defended poor people and political prisoners, too. And he was getting more and more revolutionary.

After Batista seized the power and Fidel's brief was thrown out of court, he started training and planning for the raid on Moncada. He had about 170 men and those two girls with him, most of them students, and with them he attacked those 1,000 Batista soldiers there in that fort. He was trying to take them by surprise, get their guns, and go on the radio to call up the people against the dictator.

As a military job, it didn't work out—although as the first act of the insurrection it did work, as everyone now knows. Some were killed in the attempt; some were captured and tortured in the Batista way; some were held for trial. But most of those that got killed were just murdered after the attack was all over. It was the real beginning of the Batista blood bath, of the trigger-happy Batistas roaming the streets and shooting off their guns at us.

Fidel and his brother, Raul, and some others, were put on trial, if you could call it that, and then put into the prison on the Isle of Pines. But now the people came to know the great speech Fidel made, "History Will Absolve Me," smuggled out of the closed trial by shorthand reporters. But you'll have to read that somewhere else. If you've got any good publishers in North America, maybe you can, for it's one of the great works of the Americas.

We can't tell you in these letters all that happened then. But it is very well worth knowing because it shows what kind of young men these were. After seven months of solitary confinement, Fidel set up a school for the other prisoners, teaching philosophy and history himself, and studying English and reading all of José Martí again. But the people kept shouting to Batista to free Fidel, and so, to try to make himself popular—something Batista wanted, and needed!—the Fidelistas were let out of jail. They had been prisoners for about two years.

Very soon they went to Mexico; very soon they started training there, under a Cuban they found who knew from his days in Spain how to fight like a guerrilla. Colonel Alberto Bayo was his name, and he was running a little furniture factory in Mexico City. He got hold of a ranch in Chalco and they all went into training there. In Mexico, they met Ché Guevara, and others, and in 1956 when they had 82 men, they got on a small yacht and came to invade Cuba.

It was another disaster, that November, this time worse than the July at Moncada. They got lost; they missed their connection with the men waiting for them in Cuba; they bogged down in a terrible shore swamp; they were attacked. It ended up with just twelve men on top of a mountain in the Christmas of 1956. These twelve men had made it, and so Fidel said to them: "The days of the dictatorship are numbered!"

Maybe *that* was the turning point of the Cuban revolution. Because—everyone knows it now—Fidel was right.

II

Here were a few middle-class students and intellectuals in contact with the tragedy of Cuban poverty and corruption, responding to it in a revolutionary way. Of course, our Cuban intelligentsia as a whole was split. Many intellectuals were with the tyranny; many others, after some education, just wanted to forget Cuba and they left the country. They went to New York or to Miami to study, and some of these came back to become technicians or lawyers; or they tried to get jobs in the foreign ministry of Cuba so they could live abroad. Others went to Paris to study, and some of these stayed away from Cuba. In Cuba there was no cultural and intellectual life for them.

Some who came back to Cuba or who stayed here just kept quiet and tried to live as best they could. They were not any coherent circle or class or group, you understand. They were divided, and certainly they did not as a class make the revolution. As a whole they hadn't the stomach for revolution, and they were afraid somebody would put a label on them as Communists.

But a small group of young intellectuals, we were the ones who started it up. We weren't afraid of labels; we knew what we were and what we were not. Now there is one thing that you North Americans must understand about these young intellectuals, about us who led the insurrection and who are now putting through the Cuban revolution:

Since we did not belong to the old left intelligentsia—the older men who had gone through Communism and been disillusioned with Stalinism and with the purges and the trials and the 35 years of all that—we've had one enormous advantage as revolutionaries. We've not gone through all that terribly destructive process; we have not been wounded by it; and so we are free. We are revolutionaries of the post-Stalin era; we've never had any "God That Failed." We just don't belong to that lineage. We don't have all that cynicism and futility about what we're doing, and about what we feel must be done.

That is one big secret of the Cuban revolutionary.

As young intellectuals, of course, we know something about all that disillusioning process from books, and now we are studying it some—when we have the time to study—but we never lived it. We are new men. That is why we are so original and so spontaneous and so unafraid to do what must be done in Cuba. There are no ex-radicals among us. We are new radicals. We really are, we think, a new left in the world. A left that has never suffered from all that Stalinism has meant to the old left all over the world. We know only from books the Stalinist executions and the trials and the labor camps, but it doesn't touch us personally. We are without any of that ideological background; so we've had the courage for revolution; it wasn't destroyed by the terrible history of the world decline of the old left. We are people without bad memories. So we've paid attention to what was before our eyes, to the realities of Cuba. We've been able to do what must be done without the fear that all this instils in so many. And we remain free to carry on our revolution.

III

We are middle class—we didn't come from the peasantry or the workers in the city. But it was with the peasantry that we got into real touch. In some part, this was because of the military situation: the rural areas, and above all the mountains, were the only places where you could fight well against an army. You must also realize that these "peasants" were really a sort of agricultural wage worker, who, most of the year, were unemployed.

Every revolution exaggerates the evils of the old order. We Cubans have not had to do that. In its very realities, the rural order of the old Cuba was an exaggeration—an exaggeration of social hell. It was a place of unrelieved poverty and without hope.

As we will explain to you later, the old Cuba was the exploited object of what we call Yankee imperialism. In addition to that, our own economy was a robber's capitalism, full of waste and tied together by bribery, by graft, and by plain and fancy thievery. Our politics was a corrupt copy of a constitutional democracy—it was nether constitutional nor democratic. It was a tyranny, resting squarely upon the army, and used economically by the tyrant and his henchmen for their own personal enrichment. Before, when we were making the insurrection, we didn't know everything about all this. The one thing we knew was the result of it all, and that was easy to see: poverty. This poverty was a settled condition, felt personally as a total absence of any future.

In our Caribbean paradise of violence and grief, of terror and misery, almost nine out of ten of the rural "homes" (although North Americans would hardly call our *bohíos* "homes") had only kerosene lighting. Less than 3 percent had water piped into them. More than half did not even have—perhaps it is difficult for you to imagine this—over half did not have even an *outdoor* privy; only about 3 percent had toilets indoors.

Almost two-thirds of our children were *not* in any elementary school; and most of those who did start in school soon dropped out. In 1950, for example, 180,000 children began the first grade, but less than 5,000 began the eighth grade. That figure is not for the countryside only; it is for the whole of Cuba, city and country.

Every year to this rural misery and sloth came the *tiempo muerto,* the dead season, and then the field hands and the mill workers were hungry. Because of the short season of work in the cane fields and in the sugar mills, and because sugar was such a dominating crop, and because nothing was done about it all, Cubans were without any work for months out of every year.

In the middle of the economic boom that North America got out of the Korean war, the Cuban census revealed that for the whole of Cuba on any average day one fourth of our workers and peasants were unemployed. As two of your own economists have pointed out, this fact about Cuba means that every Cuban year was like the *worst* year of your big depression in the 1930's. For us, that was "normal," and please do not insult us by asking about unemployment insurance or relief; these, as they say, were for rich Yankees. Unemployment in Cuba was chronic and unrelieved.

It was the result of our history, this miserable poverty. In the middle of your riches, maybe it is difficult for you to know what poverty is. Poverty is mean, Yankee, in case you've forgotten, or if you never knew, poverty is dreary. It is a way of dying yet not dying. Poverty means no shoes, and the rich, fat worms crawling in the intestines of your children, up through the naked soles of their feet. Poverty in Cuba meant eight people existing —who could say living?—in a miserable, filthy shack, with a floor of dirt, a leaking roof of thatch, and open fires to cook on, huddling around, coughing in the smoke.

And these, these are the people our learned young men joined up with, and mobilized, to make our revolution. Know that well: these people are the base, the thrust, the power. It is from them that the rebel soldiers came. They are the revolutionaries.

IV

But it was not this old economic order—no matter how bad—that "made" the Cuban revolution. The result of that economy—abject poverty—of course was a real cause of our action, and immediately we succeeded we began to remake and to expand the whole economy of Cuba, from top to bottom.

But the revolution itself was not a fight between peasants and landowners, or between wage workers and capitalists—either Cuban or Yankee; nor was it a direct nationalist battle between Cubans and any foreigners.

It is not an "economically determined" revolution—either in its origins or in its course. As it has come to grips with the economic facts of life, the revolution has overrun them, leaving in its immediate wake new economic facts of life.

Our revolution is not a revolution made by labor unions or wage workers in the city, or by labor parties, or by anything like that. It is far from any revolution you ever heard of before. First of all, as we've already told you, its leaders have been young intellectuals and students from the University of Havana. They were the ones who made the first moves. They made a lot of first moves for a long time before some of their moves began to pay off. Then, as they moved, the movement they were building picked up the power of the Cuban peasants, of the *campesinos*. Our revolution really began—and the fate of Batista was sealed—when a handful of these young intellectuals really got together with the peasants. That active, historical juncture did it.

And along with that, the way the rebel soldiers combined military action and economic revolution in the countryside, during the insurrection, and now afterward.

So far as the different classes of Cuba are concerned, the revolution looks like this: Throughout, it has been, and it is, led by this young intelligentsia. But there are two phases—the second still going on.

The first phase is the insurrection. Here, there is no doubt about it, the peasants played the big role. Together with the young intellectuals, they became the

rebel army that won the insurrection. They were the decisive ones, the intellectuals and the *campesinos*.

At that time, the wage workers in the city were not
conscious in any revolutionary way; their unions were
merely like your North American unions: out for more
money and better conditions. That was all that really
moved them. And some were even more corrupt than
some of yours.

The Cuban middle class, what there was of it, was
partly corrupted too. They had some organs of middle-
class expression, but they did not have any class consciousness, not even a rudimentary consciousness. Certainly, they left the Cuban peasant to rot, out in the
backward areas of Cuba. They resisted Batista and crit-
icized him sometimes, and they grumbled, often only because they were not let in on things, but they failed
completely to do anything real about the Batista tyranny.

Phase two is the revolution itself, beginning after our
insurrection triumphed at the end of 1958. Since then
the peasants have remained decisive, but now the wage
workers have become very important too. They too have
joined the revolution. It's been amazing to see how the
consciousness of the Cuban wage worker has been trans-
formed from the old trade unionism to a radical revolutionary condition. In Cuba today, of course, that means
not only "to be *for* the revolution," in some abstract way;
it means to make sacrifices for it, actively to help it
move on. And that the wage workers have done and are
doing. Because of this the revolution has become
much stronger and more radical; its velocity has been
increased by the wage workers. Their revolutionary consciousness is aroused; now it is a reality. Now they, as
well as the peasants, are an essentially revolutionary
class; now they, too, are in full revolutionary cry. But
it wasn't like that at first.

When the 26th of July finally came to Havana, after
the triumph, we revolutionaries told the wage workers:
"You didn't make it; we made the revolution, not you;
and so now you must be doubly militant to make up
for that." And that is what they have been. For example,
the wage workers have donated 4% from their wages to
buy farm machinery for the country, and many times in

the country we have seen tractors being given by different wage-worker groups to the peasants. The labor movement has definitely joined the revolution and is now a firm part of it.

And the middle classes in general? Where do they stand today? As usual, they are split and they waver and they are often frightened. Many, of course, especially the professional people—and especially schoolteachers and medical doctors—are with and for the revolution. But the middle classes are also one source of counterrevolutionary sentiment. It is good for the revolution, we think, that Cuba's middle class was never what is called a classic bourgeoisie—never strong and growing. Of course, when we first triumphed, many of them were very glad—not so much that we had won, but that Batista was done with. But as the revolution really got under way, it affected some of them in their pocketbooks and more of them in their bourgeois hearts. But we'll write to you about the counterrevolution some other time.

Let's get back to phase one, the insurrection. It's true we do like very much to think about that; it's true those who fought then, they are the ones we honor and trust the most now. You can understand that, can't you?

We rebel soldiers, formed of peasants and led by young intellectuals, we didn't just defeat an organized army; we destroyed it, once and for all. The fight against Batista's army, trained and supplied by you, that was the most important fight. As we've told you, it was certainly more important than any "class struggle" between wage workers and property owners, either foreign or Cuban. The landowners and the industrialists were not so powerful. They were strongest in agriculture, and that power was quite easy to break up once Batista's army was broken up. In fact, it just evaporated.

Everyone had always thought that you couldn't make a revolution without winning over the professional army. But we won against the army, and now there is no professional army in Cuba. The first thing we did upon winning was to turn the six biggest army garrisons in Cuba into schools, and now the Pentagon of the old Cuba is the Ministry of Education. If we had just beat the army and left them around, by now they'd have made a *coup d'état,* or tried to. But we smashed them to bits and ran them away for good.

Our rebel soldiers—they don't like being called just "soldiers"—are of a different class entirely from the old Batista army. They are a new kind of army: they aren't just sitting around military garrisons and strutting along the streets. They are working. They are building poultry houses and roads into the most backward areas of Cuba; they are going to school; they are planting tens of thousands of young eucalyptus trees on land that used to be just wasteland.

We don't want to leave you with the impression that it was only the peasant rebel soldiers who won the insurrection. There was an underground in the city, too, and many of our brothers worked there and died there for the revolution. But the conditions in the city were very bad, very unfavorable for the revolution; it was a police tyranny there, not like up in the mountains.

About seven months before we finally won, there was a strike in the city, which failed. That failure meant that all the military forces of the tyranny were turned against those of us who were up in the mountains. Those forces came up to our mountains and tried, once and for all, to kill us off. Do you know how many armed men we had then? About 300. That was all we had—and that, Yankee, maybe that was the turning point of the Cuban revolution.

V

Thirteen army teams, each 900 men strong, came towards the mountains.

Twelve thousand men paid by Batista—the biggest troop movement, they say, in the history of Cuba—in trucks, jeeps, trains, moved toward the mountains.

From Fort Moncada and the base at Bayamo, Sherman tanks—supplied by you, Yankee—clanked towards the mountain.

And we waited for them all—in our log and earth

bunkers—supplied by *us*, Yankee. We dug tank traps; we blew up bridges on highway and railroad; we hid in trees, ready to snipe; we were in our Sierra Maestra, in the jungle, on the cliff, up the gorge.

First came the planes, with napalm bombs—supplied by you, Yankee. Then the troops came into our woods— and one thing we can do is shoot accurately. They couldn't. They got tired too quick; they were flabby; and they couldn't shoot worth a damn. The officers who commanded them were just plain stupid, too. They didn't have iron faces, but they had wooden heads. Maybe we shouldn't say that, seeing as how your Military Missions had helped train them, but it's true.

The Batistas brought along some of your bazookas, too, but what did we have for them to shoot at? Nothing. So we captured the bazookas and we shot their tanks with them. We captured their tanks, too, when their crews abandoned them in the gasoline-fired tank traps we had fixed up along the trail.

And then we captured one of their portable radio senders—*with* their code book! And then, my friend, we really mixed them up. Then we knew what they were ordered to do, so we cut their supply line. Over their own radio we ordered their own bombers to strafe and bomb their own positions. We had their planes parachute supplies *to us*. Oh, then we ate the meat from cans, and cheese, and the guava jelly cakes. Mother of God, those cakes were good, after only scraps of meat and yams and not much of that for months and months.

So here's the story of the insurrection in one sentence: a handful of men on a mountain top, half starving at that, defeated a 12,000-man army paid by Batista and largely supplied and trained by Yankees. Nobody paid us, we who fought against all that army. We had other things to fight for. Nobody trained us, either. We trained ourselves as we went along, up in the hills, and later on the plains. We young men of the 26th of July Movement who mobilized the peasants, we were not like other middle-class young men. We were not out just for ourselves; we were not closed up in our own little interests. We were not disillusioned and made cynical by revolutionary defeats elsewhere in the world. We had big objectives that went beyond our own little interests and beyond all the old futilities. We were above all of that; we just didn't care about it. We represented Cuba, and so we won.

VI

Then what happened? We know the pictures you've seen—of Cubans shooting Cubans. And they're true. We executed Batistas, about five or six hundred. Killed them dead, without what North Americans would consider— rather curiously, we think—"a fair trial." We know you say you don't like this, so we want to explain to you something about how we see it.

This *was* a war. During the Batista regime, thousands of our people were murdered. Those people we rebel soldiers executed were the worst criminals of the Batista tyranny; we all knew them well. So what would you expect?

Maybe in easy moral terms, *no* killing is excusable, including—please remember—the enormous slaughters of the wars you Yankees have been in. But however immoral, the purposes and the results of killing are quite different in different places and at different times. Because, you see, it does matter who is getting killed and why. That again never excuses the killing as such; as Christians, we know that—but it does give different meanings to different killings—and the Cuban killings we think were just and necessary killings.

But whether you think so or not, you certainly have no grounds for talking about injustice: Who gave any trial to the people of Hiroshima? Well, this, too, was a war.

Remember, too, Yankee, that morals are easy to come by sitting in your quiet suburbs away from it all, protected from it all. Morals are easy to say out when you're rich and strong and all the unpleasantnesses of the world are hidden from you—by distance, by amusements, by your own indifference, by your own private way of life.

But come down to the history, the history you *are* now a part of, that history is cruel—for others. Come down to Cuba. History in Cuba has been very cruel indeed. We are trying, don't you see, to end the injustice and cruelty that had been built down into our very way of life—and with which you have had quite something to do, Yankee.

But here's the most important thing you ought to know. By the execution of the worst Batista hoodlums, and the putting into jail of other war criminals, Fidel and his rebel soldiers saved Cuba from a blood bath. Do you know that Fidel Castro and his men went on the radio and said to the people: "Act with revolutionary restraint; you will have justice." If he hadn't done that the Cuban people would have made a blood bath in Cuba. And we people are grateful to him now for having saved us from doing that; but at the time, we were mad to the point of frenzy; we would have killed them all, and maybe *then* there would have been injustices done.

Maybe you've heard some ex-Cuban businessman telling you that he is against Fidel Castro *because* of these executions. That's a counterrevolutionary theme song today all over the *business* world. What does it mean? It means that our revolution has shown up in their balance books. What this kind of Cuban wanted was a nice, safe little democracy, with the old Latin American graft out of it, so that the more impersonal and hidden Yankee kind of graft could be carried on more neatly, more cleanly, more systematically.

You still think, Yankee, that it's the morals of the executions they're all against? Why, then, was there no organized propaganda among these people or by the newspapers and radios and magazines they control when the Batistas were doing the killing? There wasn't; there was just the opposite: your Government sent its military men down to our island to help train the Batistas, who were doing the killing then. Your Government gave them guns and planes and bombs and trained the Batistas to use all these against us. Think about that, Yankee, when you think about our firing squads.

For so long as Batista ruled, your business and your government were directly and indirectly a part of his rule and you made no protest. On the contrary: you helped him. Even when we Fidelistas won you did not protest. You could hardly afford to. It was so obvious that we Cubans were overjoyed.

But the minute we began to organize for our own use corporation property—Cuban as well as Yankee, please note—then your newspapers, your Yankee Government, all your radios came out hard and loud against us. Your State Department screamed, your radios bellowed, and very soon you cut the Cuban sugar quota. You didn't help our revolution. You've never helped it. You hurt it. And now you're trying to shut it down, to kill it off; you're trying to hurt us more and more. So that is why we do shout out loud, to the world and to you:

"Cuba, sí!

"Yankee, no!"

But if we are wrong about this maybe you can prove it to us? It should be easy for you. You're a democracy, aren't you?

T H R E E

YOUR COUNTERREVOLUTION

Every revolution has its counterrevolution—that is a sign the revolution is for real. And every revolution must defend itself against this counterrevolution, or the revolution will fail. Nowadays, in countries like ours, counterrevolutions are almost always supported from abroad, certainly the counterrevolution to our revolution is supported from abroad. Some of the things we're going to tell you now we can't prove. By their very nature, that's impossible. But maybe you could look into it, Yankee, and help us know more about it, so we could defend ourselves better. Who are the counterrevolutionaries? And what kind of power do they have?

I

First of all, they are the Batistas who are now in exile mainly in the United States. They have plenty of money, which they stole from Cuba, and we do believe that they plot mightily against our revolution. They go to the United States because their only chance of stopping our revolution rests on their hope that your Government will somehow help them against us. You have now in your country many thugs and gangsters of the Batista regime; some of them are even asked to testify before your Congressional committees. Inside Cuba, they certainly don't have any force or prestige. The system they represent is so drenched with blood; they themselves represent to us such crime and poverty—they have nothing to say to us. They are depending upon your ignorance and upon your just not caring.

Along with these Batistas are The Defectors—men who were with the revolution for a while but then deserted it. They have quit the revolution and, in fact.

they have quit Cuba. Most of these too have gone to your country. Who are they? Perhaps you know some of their names, but what else do you know about them? There was, for example, Huber Matos—once a *commandante* who fought with Fidel; that was the biggest blow. There was Diaz Lanz—head of the air force—he fought in the hills, too; Raul Chibas of the rebel army, and brother of Eduardo Chibas. There was Miguel A. Queredo, the publisher of our magazine, *Bohemia,* and Luis Conte Agüero—a radio man now in Miami; and Miro Cardona—a former ambassador to the United States, with money in the banks all over.

Each of these men, and the others, had his own reason for deserting the revolution, although almost all of them gave anticommunism as the reason. That's the big counterrevolutionary theme song, of course. None of them, except perhaps one or two, was really popular in Cuba. Some were ambitious in the old political way, and then came to see that there wasn't going to be any more of that kind of politics in Cuba. Some had some property and income and lost it by the revolutionary laws; maybe that is a reason. (Fidel's own family property was, of course, cut down to size, like everyone else's.) Some defectors overestimated themselves greatly, and when they couldn't get as high in the revolutionary Government as they thought they should, they quit. At least one thought he should have been made the President of Cuba. And some, after all, were mercenaries and not very intelligent ones at that.

There's one thing about all these defectors that has to do with the kind of revolution ours happens to be: it didn't go on for very long with very many people in it; so in the revolutionary process we didn't get a chance to select and to develop very many tried and true revolutionaries. It wasn't like the French revolution, or the Chinese revolution that went on for years and years. We triumphed very quickly, by defeating an army in just two years, really. It was sooner than we expected, and that's why the revolution has lacked reliable men who know how to do what has to be done and who keep doing it. So, to some extent, these defectors are a result, we think, of our making the revolution without any long revolutionary process.

But all that's not so important to us now; those defectors just didn't have the real revolutionary stuff in them. What is important is that The Batistas who got away and The Defectors who ran off—they will, of course, try to make the counterrevolution. Most of them certainly don't have the courage to become military men themselves. But they are conspiring against us and we believe that Yankee interests and your Yankee Government is helping them do this. We believe they are all working alongside the Yankee Government. Why do we think that?

What they are doing must cost millions of dollars—their propaganda against us, their traveling, their very maintenance, and we think too, their buying of weapons. Now, some of the Batista men have money, which they stole from Cuba, but many others do not have any money; and anyone who knows the Batistas as we do knows that *they* are not giving money to anybody. Certainly they do not get money from Batista himself. So we ask ourselves, where's all the money coming from? From Yankee corporations hurt by our revolution? From your CIA? From your Department of State? Certainly none of them is popular enough among Cuban communities abroad for them to raise money there. We know some of them see your State Department officials. So we think Yankees must be helping them.

If we are wrong about this, prove it to us. Have your Congress investigate the whole counterrevolution. Can't you do that? All we want is the whole truth about it all. Until you make that whole truth clear, we'll have to keep on believing what we've said.

II

But how about counterrevolutionary sentiment *inside* Cuba? Does it exist? Yes, of course it does. Generally it's held by people who benefited from the old regime but not from the revolution and are still here—most of

the big Cuban landowners (*Latifundistas,* we call them),
for example—people directly affected in the pocketbook
by the revolutionary laws.

Every revolutionary law has naturally left in its wake
defection, resentment, and counterrevolutionary sentiment. Certainly this is true among the big latifundistas—
left in the wake of the agrarian reform—yet many of
these big owners have stayed in Cuba. The owners of
real estate, of the many big apartment houses, for example—for that was a big source of investment in the
old days for the bribers and the bribed, as well as other
capitalist profiteers—they have been hurt economically
by our low-rent laws. The gambling interests, as well as
other tourist industries, and also such Cuban "profit-
making" industries as the numbers game, the lottery, the
slot-machine racket, those who were in on the casinos.
And also, of course, all the business people who depended upon the import trade with your companies
—that's choked off, now.

Yes, many "business interests"—some real, and some
criminal—have been affected by the revolution. After
all, in the old order about one billion dollars of state
money was invested in the political-capitalism racket.
Most of that has been taken back now by our Government, and that means: counterrevolutionary sentiment.
But let us explain to you something about these people
who are affected in this way.

Look briefly at one type of Cuban businessman in the
political-capitalism racket of the old order—or, rather,
ex-Cuban businessman. Perhaps he is living now in
Miami; he can well afford to do so. If you ask him—
"What about Cuba?"—he is likely to tell you something
like this:

"At first I was all for Castro. True, I didn't get a gun
and fight alongside him, that wasn't my job. But I was
glad he was winning. But now I am against Fidel Castro
and the revolution he is making in Cuba. He has gone
too far, much too far. I suppose down there in Cuba
they'd call me a counterrevolutionary, and perhaps I
am; except, I'd much rather say that I am for The True
Revolution, and therefore I am against what Fidel and
his bearded men are doing. The old Cuba, I suppose it

really was a bad place. Perhaps Fidel was right about
that. Yet somehow, despite everything they may say,
I liked it. A man could make plenty money there, and
spend it well, too."

The question, of course, is not, Wasn't there after all
something good about the old order? The question is—
Good for whom? The answer is, good for this sort of
man. But how did he make money in the old Cuba? You
must first realize that the old Cuba was not a capitalist
society with a strong, honest and flourishing middle
class. Cuba was just a factory. And the economic powers
in it clustered around the United States monopolies
that operated in Cuba. From inside, it was a political
capitalism; from outside, it was an imperialist colony.

Big *Cuban* fortunes were invested in sugar and banking
and real estate, but especially in farming, of course.
Those were the major fields of investment. Middle-class
capital was very limited, and so the industries in which
it was invested were small. But heavier industries, re-
quiring larger investment, these were undertaken during
the fifties by the Batista government. This is how it
worked:

Politically influential men, or the relatives of such men,
would ask for a Government loan to set up a business. This private "businessman" would put up 10% to
20% of the total capital, the rest being supplied by the
Government. This private (political) man was, of course,
"the owner"; he was supposed to pay back to the Government both the principal and the interest on the money—
on paper, that is. Such heavy industry was in sugar-cane
products, metallurgical work, paper, building materials,
and some chemical plants.

The "capitalists" who got loans in this way from the
government were interested less in sound production
than in big business "deals." They would invest, say,
$200,000 for a $2,000,000 industry, and then they would
become rich by graft. They would sell to themselves a
site for the industry, for example, and they would buy
machinery, not on a sound business basis, but in order
to get a rake-off on the deal. The plants were ill-de-
signed, the equipment was not bought at economically
feasible prices. But these "investors" would sell the

products and keep the money. It was that simple. They would not pay their debts, they would take a million or so out of the business, and then they would let it collapse. Many such "businesses" never even came into actual production, and if they did their production costs were very high, higher than the profit. But they didn't care; they just took the profits.

To put it briefly, Cuban business of this sort was part of a corrupt Government, and together with that Government formed a capitalist world of rackets. Such was the political capitalism of Cuba. And such is one basis for the counterrevolution today. For we have, of course, taken over all these businesses.

III

But the fact is, there are only a few counterrevolutionaries in Cuba, and they certainly are impotent to gather any elements around them. The middle classes will have a chance now to work and to feel more connected with the country. Of course, some of these middle-class people consider only their money; money is their only country. Still, they too have some pride in our nation. They know the world now respects Cuba, and despite their counterrevolutionary sentiment this does make them glad.

Many of the professional people, certainly most of the younger ones, are with the revolution. Young lawyers are needed by the New Government, because the old juridical system, inherently a part of the old order, was thoroughly corrupt: "permits" were needed for almost everything in the way of business, and for permits you needed bribes and fixes—and all this meant money to lawyers. So did the old corporation way of business life, and many such lawyers are against the revolution. But a new juridical system must now be built and this means new and exciting work for lawyers who are with the revolution. They must do the work of building this new system. Others of them are being employed by the Government as administrators. Many architects, too, are busy building schools and houses and new

factories, and throughout the revolutionary institutions, medical personnel are working hard at a variety of
tasks, not only medical.

But that's not the whole story. There *is* fear in the
urban middle classes of being hurt economically and
politically. Such fear is less among the professional classes
than the smaller and medium-sized businessmen. Of
course, the middle classes generally supported the
revolution, at least in a passive way, during the insurrectionary period, although as a class they had little to do
with making it. But now, as we settle down to the construction of a new deal and of a new social and economic
order, many sections of the middle class vacillate and
many zigzag towards the right, towards the counterrevolution.

The old upper classes have lost their wealth and
their power and they've lost something else, too: they've
lost much of how they used to live, their style of life.
It was an easy life, in a material way. Many years
ago, perhaps 60 years ago, it was a rather fine style of
life. Of course, it was feudal, but there was some high
culture in it, and now they are surprised that it has
disappeared so quickly, almost overnight. Sometimes it
makes them panic. You see, at first they thought the
revolution was just against Batista, and so, in a way,
that it was for them. Now they know that this isn't the
case, that it's a real revolution, and when they see before
their eyes a whole nation in the process of becoming
radical it frightens them, and they don't quite know
what to do.

There's another thing, too, about the upper and the
middle classes now, but especially about the lower middle class in the cities. It's not that they've actually lost
anything material. It's that they feel they have lost a
dream. Some of them are disappointed that they cannot
have The Big Dream any more. They never had a solid
bourgeois life, but with some of them it was like the
weekly lottery. There was always the dream of winning
the $100,000. That dream, in which many lived in the old
order, is destroyed by the revolution. The dream was to
some extent on all levels, as it is in all poor countries
—it was one big reason for all the crooked slot ma-

chines all over the island. If you were poor, you dreamed with the slot machines; if you were a little better off, you dreamed of getting a license by some bribery to teach school; if you were still better off, you dreamed of the million dollars, suddenly and miraculously yours. And now that dream—all of it, on all levels—is absolutely done with. The revolution, we've told you, is a way of defining reality—the realities of Cuba and of yourself, too. And so—the loss of that crooked dream—that's another source of counterrevolutionary sentiment in Cuba today.

Anticommunism, as we've said, is the theme song of the counterrevolutionaries. The prejudice and the confusion about these words prevail only in parts of the elite and the middle classes. It still does prevail, much more widely, in the U.S.A.—doesn't it? But this propaganda, about the Cuban revolution being communist, is very clever. It does spread confusion and worry in Cuba, especially because the middle classes do not have any real orientation to social and economic reality. But remember, the revolution is very powerful. So many of the poor are with the revolution, and against U.S. policy. Also—forgive us, but it's true—U.S. policy has been and is so obviously stupid that this propaganda doesn't always work. And now, the Cuban middle classes are not so worried as they used to be.

The middle class thought at first that the revolution was merely a change of men. Now they see that it is not. It is a real revolution. Many sections of the middle class were anti-Batista, but many of them only because Batista would not let them "coexist" with him. They thought that his downfall meant the occasion for them to enjoy power and privilege. But the revolution does not mean that. It means the liquidation of privileges, so the mediocrity of these middle-class sections has now been put into evidence.

You must also realize that the interests of the middle class of the old Cuba were very much tied up with the interests—socially as well as economically and politically —of U.S. business. When power went into the hands of the people, the middle classes began to mistrust the revolution. So, naturally, in some cases, the charge that

all we Cubans are Communists—that caught the imagination of these people. Now the peasants and the wage
workers, being organized better, are creating a great
force against such lies. The moral and the cultural as-
pects of the revolution are becoming clearer, and so we
can resist this kind of psychological warfare.

IV

As far as our religion is concerned, we Cubans know
it's of no importance in the counterrevolution. That's
something Yankees are making up. Certainly inside
Cuba the Catholic faith of the people is no basis for
counterrevolutionary sentiment.

First of all, this religion isn't very deep in Cuba.
The religion of the people in the country is a curious
mixture of African cults and images with a thin layer of
Roman Catholic faith and symbols. All you have to do is
travel a few days in Cuba to see that there are *very*
few churches in the country and in the villages, and even
in the cities, for that matter.

The Church has not had any land, to speak of, in
Cuba. It has had neither economic nor political power
here. And certainly the clergy has not been and is not
now very widely respected. The very word for "clergy"
used so frequently in Cuba is not a very good word.
Perhaps that is because most of the clergy in Cuba
are not even Cubans. They are from Franco's Spain. Did
you know that? Some say 800 of the 1,000 clergy are not
Cubans at all.

As far as the more educated people are concerned,
the generation of the thirties—those who are about 50
today—many of them went to Catholic schools; and, if
they were leftist, they were also anticlerical. That was
part of how they grew up. It was often in the religious
crisis of their adolescence that they became leftists of
some sort. But that's all over now. It doesn't *mean*
anything to be anticlerical. Their children are neither
Catholic nor anti-Catholic. It just doesn't matter to
them. It's irrelevant. They are for Cuba, and so they are
for the revolution. They did not come to that by be-

coming radical, much less anti-Catholic. They just grew up in that state of revolutionary grace.

Maybe that's one reason why when those bishops came out with a general declaration against "communism," so many of our people in the churches laughed it off so easily. They knew it was just the ignorance and the fear of counterrevolutionaries. Our people know that our leaders aren't "communists." In Manzanillo, for example, in August 1960, that bishop's statement was read at the 7 o'clock Mass, but then at the 9 o'clock Mass the people shouted it down; they didn't want to hear all that. Our real religion in Cuba is for the Cuban revolution; we don't want any religion that's counterrevolutionary.

V

You must realize, too, that we are armed against counterrevolution. We have not only our rebel soldiers, but also our citizens' militia, who are formed in our cooperatives and Government farms and in all our city enterprises, too. We don't forget that there are many of Batista's ex-soldiers still walking around Cuba. We are all in training and each man knows what to do. You might well say that, among other things, we are an armed camp against the counterrevolution. Our rebel soldiers and our reserve militia are not like most armies. We come from the farmers and the workers, and now we've got guns in our hands and the revolutionary orientation in our hearts and minds. We are not only good soldiers, we are good revolutionaries, too. We are in very close touch with the interests of all the people. We *are* the people in arms. We know our cause is just, we're not in the army for the money. And we're going to school, almost all of us rebel soldiers, and learning much more than just how to fight. We are an army that is working at every task we can work at. Because: Revolution is construction. And from our schools and also from the very way we're living and working in the revolution, we are learning how to defend our revolution and all the gains that we've made.

So ours, we think, is not like any other army in the world. It's a working army and an army going to school. Those of us who are rebel soldiers work directly with INRA—an organization we'll tell you about later—in construction and planting trees and everything else INRA is doing. Of course, you must realize that we feel we are forced to be something of an armed camp of a nation, but that isn't stopping us from our educational and economic construction. We're supplementing our rebel army with militia, too. Every cooperative, every enterprise of any sort, has its own militia, and each man knows what to do in case of emergency.

VI

So we Cuban revolutionaries don't worry much about counterrevolution *inside* Cuba. What we do worry about—and it's making us do many of the things we are doing—is you. We think the United States is somehow going to try to stop our revolution, directly or indirectly. As we see it: the only possibly effective counterrevolutionary force is the United States of America. We're not afraid of this, we're not afraid of anything, but we do know that we have to prepare well to meet it. When we shout "My country or my death!" we mean just that—and we are shouting it to your Yankee Government and corporations because *that's* the real counterrevolutionary force against us.

But again, we say to *you*—if we're wrong about this—prove it to us; look into it; look into it before it is too late for us all. In the meantime, we've your own history to go on and we'll stick to that. Forget the old history we've already told you about. Think about only yesterday and today:

Your Government is protecting in the U.S.A. war criminals from the old Batista regime. Probably your CIA is recruiting some of them as agents. At least, your Government is providing safe refuge for them while they plot to harass our work and quite possibly to invade us. You have them "testify" before your Congressional committee. Planes have flown from your territory to Cuba, some of them piloted by U.S. citizens, to inflict damage on our properties and our citizens. They've burned our refineries and cane fields. You've been arming neighboring countries, like Haiti, but you won't sell us arms. You've tried to stop us from buying arms in Europe, as well as farm machinery.

Your Government continuously threatens to choke off our economy; Yankee oil companies have refused to refine oil that we Cubans have bought and which we own; it is an attempt to stop our economy. Your Government cut the quota for Cuban sugar in an effort to do just that. You won't even sell us small planes to dust our crops; you've held up export licenses for tractors and farm machinery. Shipments of our fruit and vegetable industry have been harassed in U.S. ports, and not inspected. You've destroyed our U.S.-Cuban tourist trade with your propaganda.

Your Government makes diplomatic proclamations, and causes other governments to do so, that deny our rights as a sovereign state. Your high and mighty don't treat us as a sovereign state, but as a kind of primitive people run by some colonial office of yours instead of by a government of our own.

All this, it seems clear to us, is attempted intervention into our Cuban affairs. It is against the Charter of the United Nations. It is an imperialist attitude from beginning to end. But more than that, in our view, it is an attempted counterrevolution against us.

Since we say this—that Yankee interests and the Yankee Government is the major counterrevolutionary force we see—let us go into it a little more. Let us ask: What *can* the U.S.A. do to hurt the Cuban revolution?

Politically, we don't think they can do much against us. They can cause the Organization of American States—which we often think is generally an unwieldly colonial office of the U.S.A.—to make shaky proclamations against us. But these proclamations don't scare us, and they don't mean much. For one thing, some of those governments in the O.A.S. are pretty shaky themselves, and many of their peoples are with us; more of them will be when they come to know what we're really doing and how well off the people of Cuba are getting to be. But more important than that, these political proclamations have no economic bite, and they have no military significance either.

Do you know why? Now you're going to learn something about Yankee imperialism: The countries of Latin America, living alongside each other, do not generally have any significant economic relations with each other. Each of them has economic relations with U.S. corporations. As raw-material producers—usually producers of just one or two lines of commodities—they are each tied to you. So even if the U.S.A. gets these countries to make some kind of "economic blockade" of Cuba, it wouldn't hurt us in any real economic way. But we don't think your Government could get them even to try.

Economically, of course, the U.S. has tried to hurt us directly, but so far it has failed, and we are already beyond the point where it could hurt us in any real way. In fact, we are going very soon to be much better off in our new economic independence than we were, and much better off than most of the other Latin American countries that are still under the Yankee economic yoke.

To understand this, you have to know all about sugar and why in Cuba sugar is getting sweeter all the time. We'll tell you about that in our next letter, but briefly we've been—like other Latin American countries—tied to you by a single crop and by all your imports to us. It was because of this that we have been so poor. But now, we've got away from all that.

You tried to kill us off by cutting the sugar quota; obviously, it didn't work. You're trying to hurt us economically by not selling us parts for the machines we have that were made in the U.S.A.—but that won't work, either. The truth is, there is now nothing economic that the U.S.A.—as a set of corporations and as a government—can do to stop the revolution in Cuba. We'll try to prove that better in our next letter, but now let us ask this question: Isn't your Government really left with only one way to act against our Government and against us—military violence against Cuba?

But what kind of *military* action can the U.S. take

against us? Consider the possibilities, please, because we certainly are thinking about them every day.

The Big Way is this: if you think of military action on a war scale—as in World War II in the Pacific, say— and if no one helps Cuba, then you could defeat us. But to do that, your intervention would have to be on a really massive scale, and it could succeed only after you slaughtered over half the population of Cuba—and even then there would be resistance in the hills for a very long time, if not forever. But of course we don't feel this Big Way is so much of a threat now, as we did a little while ago: it would disgrace you before the world, but more important, certain other powers, big and little, would certainly come to the aid of Cuba. We take very seriously the Russian offer of aid if you attack us.

Now, what's the truth about this Soviet offer of coming to help us, with rockets, if need be? We think the truth is this: If the United States does *not* intend to make a military intervention in Cuba, then what does the United States care if the Soviet Union proclaims that *in such a case* Russian rockets will fly? If there is not going to be "such a case" then is not the Soviet statement irrelevant? And would not the best policy be for the U.S. to say to the world: "This Soviet statement is absurd. It is based on an illusion. The United States is not going to use military force against Cuba in any way whatever, nor support any military force of any kind against Cuba. Therefore, the Soviet statement is irrelevant nonsense. So forget about it."

Why doesn't the U.S. Government say that? Why does your Government try to get Cuba and other Latin American countries to denounce the offer of Soviet rocket aid? Why did the Russians have such a good chance to make the offer, anyway? If you can't answer those questions, then maybe you can answer this one: Why are we Cubans glad to have the protection of the Soviet offer?

What we want from the U.S.A. can be put into one word: *Nothing*. If only the fear of your military action against us, direct or indirect, if only that were removed, we'd be happy to have nothing further to do with the

U.S.A. The military truth just now, which we are living in, is that you are menacing us.

Now there is no other army but yours in the Western Hemisphere that is capable of conquering us, and we don't believe you could get any combination of Latin American nations to try to do it. But if you did, the results would be the same as in The Big Way.

There is another way that won't work either: If you tried to conquer us again, with your left hand as it were, in a kind of police action, you could damage us and set back our economic progress, but you'd take one hell of a beating too—and perhaps not only on Cuban soil. We revolutionaries know all sorts of ways to fight. Please understand that well. What you must know is that our *people* are mobilized and that we are a government—in fact, all our new institutions are filled with young men who have just come out of a war in which thousands of Cubans were killed. Death is nothing new to us. We will not flee the country as Batista did. We are determined to fight to the end. Anyone who is here in Cuba for just a little while sees clearly that this is just a fact.

So there is only one way: The most likely thing your Government is dreaming of is some kind of indirect military action, secretly supporting mercenaries and Batista henchmen; something like they did in Guatemala a while back. This intervention wouldn't come from U.S. soil, but maybe from somewhere in Central America. Maybe your counterrevolutionaries dream of conquering our Isle of Pines and setting up there some kind of counterrevolutionary "government." They know, of course, that there are war prisoners on that island— Batista people. They'd let them out. And if they had some kind of puppet regime there, they could "recognize" it and arm it. That would be their fig leaf. Then they could harass us and, of course, cause us trouble and set back our economic construction.

By the way, you don't seem to know much about the Guatemala affair, do you? We don't either, although some of us know more about it than we're in a position to tell you just now. What's plain to all is this:

The way your politicians and newspapers and secret services are acting towards Cuba now is very much like the way they acted towards Guatemala back in 1954. There a man named Juan José Arevalo abolished forced labor on the plantations, and raised wages to 26¢ a day. Right away, Yankees started their campaign of abuse and started shrieking "Communist!" The peasants demanded land. The U.S. Government, we are told, rushed arms by airplane from Panama to certain military men they trusted. Then a man named Jacobo Arbenz was elected President of Guatemala, and began taking seriously the agrarian reform and the labor laws; he even raised wages to $1.08 a day! The United Fruit Company didn't like that. The Yankee newspapers found a "red" every other day in the Arbenz government. The U.S. State Department issued a McCarthy-type statement.

We don't know how many Communists the Arbenz government had in it, but—according to your own Latin American expert, Carleton Beals—certainly no more than the governments of Chile, Italy, Bolivia, France, Brazil, or Batista's Cuba! All of those governments, according to Mr. Beals, had more Communists and stronger Communist movements than Guatemala had.

Anyway, The Inter-American Congress met and your Mr. John Foster Dulles jammed through a condemnation of Guatemala. In nearby Honduras and Nicaragua, some Guatemalans started piling up arms—among them at least one, Carlos Castillo Armas, was actually a pro-Nazi, and a great "pro-democratic" favorite of your Department of State. Guatemala tried to get the U.N. to look into all this, but nothing happened. It was Monroe Doctrine territory. So then came the *putsch*: Armas got hold of the government.

Now think about all that, please. Isn't it somewhat like the way your politicians and newspapers have been acting towards Cuba? But the ending isn't going to be the same, we can assure you of that. It won't work again. It would be too transparent; we are too well informed; and we can defend our Isle of Pines. We've got antiaircraft guns there, and everything else we need.

And wherever Fidel goes, the rebel soldiers on their posts come up to him and say: "If you hear the Isle of Pines is taken, Fidel, know that there is not one of us left alive." There is no question whatsoever in anybody's mind but that they mean this literally. All of us do. And besides, any attempt to conquer the Isle of Pines would very soon lead to the same consequence as in The Big Way.

We told you before: We are not alone any more.

But please listen to us, Yankee: Can't *you* do anything about all this before it happens? Haven't you *anything* to say about what your Government does? Can't you make your Congress look into your counterrevolution against us? Can't you, once and for all, prove to us that we are wrong about the menace of Yankee intervention? These—you must know it—are the most important questions we Cubans are going to be asking you. And every day we are waiting for your answer, every day with guns in our hands.

F O U R

DO-IT-YOURSELF ECONOMICS

The truth about what we're doing economically in Cuba is that we're a do-it-yourself outfit, and that in ev-erything we've done and are doing we've acted and we are acting without reference to ideology of any kind. We're acting with close and continual reference to one master aim: To make Cuba economically sovereign and eco-nomically prosperous.

To do this, we have to accomplish three immediate tasks, which we already have well in hand:

First, we are increasing and diversifying our produc-tion and our consumption—especially in our agriculture.

Second, we are increasing and diversifying our export markets and our sources of supply from abroad.

Third, we are beginning to industrialize our island at the same time as we are immediately improving our standard of living.

As soon as the insurrection triumphed, in January 1959, our economic revolution began, and very soon we came upon two economic institutions and one chronic economic condition. These were hard facts, inherited from the old order, and they stood in the way of our economic aims and our economic needs. The chronic condition was the poverty and the unemploy-ment; these were the basic results of the old system. That old system was made up of two institutions that stood in our way: One was imperialism, the other was entirely Cuban—it was the political capitalism of the Batista thieves we've already told you about.

We don't want to leave the impression that we knew all our aims and obstacles in so clear-cut a way from the very beginning. We didn't. We came upon one fact at a time, as we began to go to work building our economy and trying to do something about the unemployment.

71

We've tried to meet many of our problems in different ways, and many of these ways didn't seem to work, but we've kept at it. We've had to, and in working at it, we've come to our over-all aims and our plans of how to realize them.

|

But what was the "imperialism" of the old Cuba? It rested, of course, upon foreign-owned capital, which in Cuba meant Yankee-owned capital. And it wasn't only the sugar fields and the mills and the oil refineries and the electric company and the rubber-tire plants and the telephone system. It was also the preferential tariffs given to U.S. capitalists—and only to U.S. capitalists—who sold so many things to Cuba that Cubans had to have.

We've told you that we've been in poverty and that now we're coming out of poverty, but *why* have we been so poor for so long? It's a new question among us. *Now,* of course, we know we are a rich island with willing and able people; every day we are proving that. Why then were we so poor for so long?

In one word: sugar.

Of course, some Cubans have long known that it is not wise for any nation to base its very existence upon any single crop. But there wasn't anything that Cubans could do about it.

But that one word, "sugar," is not quite enough to explain the old agrarian order of Cuba. Two other words are needed: "Imperialism" and "Monopoly." And both these words meant the same things—the concentration of our riches in the hands of just a few people, the misuse of our land, and much land not being used at all, and certainly not much use of our labor power.

In the old order, in the countryside, there was no middle class to speak of. There were the few rich, usually absentee owners—some Cuban and some Yankee—and then there was the great mass of the utterly poor.

Just after the Second World War, less than one-tenth of all the farms in Cuba held over two-thirds of the land. Our soil and climate are among the best in the world; you can grow almost anything in it. But we could not even grow enough to feed ourselves. Yet we were not overpopulated. The fact is simple: We couldn't use our land for the kind of diversified agriculture we needed. We had to import at high prices we simply couldn't afford 70% of all we ate. Again, why? Again: sugar.

Until 1934, the United States companies that bought Cuban sugar paid the same price as the companies of all other countries. But in that year, the quota system was established by the U.S. It was designed to protect your producers of beet sugar in the U.S. A tariff was not enough to do this, for these U.S. producers could not compete on the world market. So by the quota system, the U.S.A. withdrew from the world market, setting up special prices higher than this market. The quota assigned to sugar producers in Cuba was lower than what they had been exporting to the U.S. Cuba could have sold more sugar at a free price in the U.S. and elsewhere. But many Cubans then supposed that this lesser amount was made up for by the higher price. The higher price has been maintained since 1934—although in some periods the price of sugar paid by the U.S. buyers has been lower than the world price: for example, during World War II and the Korean and Suez crises.

Many people think that the U.S. was making a present to Cuba by this quota price. But we think the fact is that this higher price was not enough to make up for the balance of payments between the U.S. and Cuba. In other words, you have to look not only at the sales in sugar, but at *all* the economic transactions between Cuba and the U.S.A.

When you do that, you see at once that in return for the sugar quota, as it were, U.S. *exporters* to Cuba got a highly privileged status—the preferential tariffs. This preferential status gave the U.S. exporters to Cuba such an advantage that no one else could compete with them. Producers of sugar *in* Cuba were given a higher import price, but by an advantageous tariff, U.S. exporters *to* Cuba took back any benefit the quota system might have produced. (All tariffs are bilateral, of course, but the

U.S. Senate can unilaterally change the Cuban quota for sugar. They have now done so, in the early summer of 1960.)

In the ten years preceding the triumph of our revolution, in spite of the higher price paid for sugar, the balance of payment was negative for Cuba. A total of some $100 million per year was involved. Cuba gave concessions in tariffs and taxes to the U.S. companies, which thus dominated the Cuban import market. Cubans could not buy elsewhere. In the last ten years of the tyranny, despite its tiny economy, Cuba lost some one billion dollars to the United States.

To this must be added the fact that about 40% of Cuba's sugar production was in the hands of the U.S. corporations. (There was a time when it was as high as 60%, but in the 1930's, U.S. producers let go of the little mills they had owned and kept only the big ones.) Now, of course, all sugar is produced in *Cuban* mills, and so the economic benefit of *all* Cuban sales is Cuba's.

The U.S. economic aggression in cutting the sugar quota is only temporary in its effect. When we overcome it still further, by diversifying our exports and our imports, we will be much better off than we were in the old order, under the Yankee yoke.

But this U.S. reduction of the Cuban sugar they buy *could* have been very harmful to us. About one-fifth of Cuba's production was involved. We might have had to dump that on the world market, or we might have had to limit our production. If we dumped it, the price of sugar would go down. If we cut our production, we would have had more unemployment. Either way, this would have weakened us; it might well have been a terrific economic blow. Your Department of State was sure, we believe, that cutting the quota was going to wreck our revolutionary Government.

You must realize, then, that the Russians and the Chinese and the Japanese have saved Cuba much hardship and perhaps economic catastrophe by buying our sugar. But in two to four years we will not be dependent on the Russian market. For Cuba's international quota for sugar has already gone up, because the world demand for sugar is going up. One reason for this is that the Soviet countries are buying sugar. And that is because their standard of living is increasing. There is thus a rational economic relation between these Soviet countries and countries such as Cuba. With the Russians buying our sugar, the U.S. will have to buy one million tons, or probably even more, in the world market. And so the greater demand in the world market will increase the price of sugar. In fact, it is already going up. In the end, the Yankee consumer will suffer from this cutting of the Cuban quota—indeed, from our economic independence in general. We are no longer under the exploitative Yankee yoke. We are diversifying and we are stabilizing the market for our sugar. But of course we are not depending only on sugar. We are going to export many other things, too.

So the Yankee cut in the Cuban sugar quota is going to turn out to be of benefit to us. We have, of course, as Fidel Castro said last June (1960), "exchanged quota for investments." The Cubans lost the sugar quota; the Yankees lost their sugar investments. Well, what would you expect? In this, we did act very cautiously. We did not shout about these North American investments, or even about the import privileges North Americans had in Cuba—not until your Congress and then your President started talking big about the sugar quota and about Communists.

We're not going to sit and be exploited and manipulated by your sugar interests and their front men. And we are not alone. There are other markets for Cuban products; there are other sources of supply for the things Cubans need. We will trade with as many different countries as we possibly can. We do not care what their politics are. The more countries we sell to, and the more countries we buy from, the freer we will be, economically and politically. José Martí said it. Now we are doing it.

II

But it wasn't only Yankee imperialism and the sugar economy the revolution had to correct. We also had to put the old political capitalism of Batista in order. Some 80% of the capital in our industries was Government money, and most of the "owners" were henchmen of Batista. We would have confiscated these properties because of the Batista connection alone, quite apart from the simple economic justice of taking them over. All "businesses" set up in this way of the thief, we took over. Whenever we found clean private money in industry, that capital investment we recognized, and most of those owners have stayed on as partners, owning whatever percentage was rightly theirs. But most of the Cuban industry set up during the fifties was the Batista sort of robber capitalism. Since our triumph, some businesses have gone bankrupt, and so we have taken them over in order to keep them running. We've done this to keep employment up. Most industries now held by the Government have come from this group and from the Batista group directly.

Our principle here is to keep industry going even if it is not, at the moment, economically sound. This, of course, is an indirect subsidy to the wage worker. When we triumphed in January 1959, 700,000 were unemployed. We've already reduced it by 200,000. But we still have half a million people unemployed. And this unemployment is still one of our main economic worries. The people have a low purchasing power and also 45% of them are farmers. The average farmer's family has six persons in it, and a monthly income of about $40. Again, our immediate unemployment limits the degree to which we can make our industry more technically efficient, or rationalize it. If we rationalize the sugar industry, for example, we could sell sugar at a much lower price than we do. Nonetheless, we've already modernized the sugar mills, and concentrated the 160 mills into fewer, larger productive facilities. Our low standard of living also reduces the size of our internal market, but as we'll explain in a minute, this will be helped a lot—and immediately—by the agrarian reform. The problem is how we can industrialize our island if half our population hasn't yet got adequate purchasing power. That is why the agrarian reform is our main economic step—it immediately brings up the standard of living.

III

On the 17th of May, 1959, our agrarian reform law was signed, and Fidel Castro gave Commandante Vallejo, INRA Head in the province of Oriente, a check for $100,000, and said to him, "Produce!" There were no further instructions. First, the Commandante made a list of all the big farms in the area, and the first day he took over two of them. The people working there asked, "What do you want us to do?" and the Commandante said, "Well, I don't really know." And the people said, "We will plant some beans." And that is what they did. It began like that. No force was used in the interventions; it wasn't necessary.

We have taken over property according to its size; that is what our law says. We leave the small owners alone, but if they are not in higher production within a year or two, we will have to intervene there too. But now we are helping these little ones. We think small land owners will naturally join into larger cooperatives. They form committees and these *are* cooperatives in almost all senses of the word. For example, the other day, in August 1960, 700 small owners in corn production came together. If they have high enough production for them to keep their land individually, then they will keep it. But we revolutionaries do prefer cooperatives, because then medical and social and educational facilities are easier to fix up for the people. So we try to get them to see the good results of this pooling of their land. We are looking to production, see? Organization is more or less taking care of itself.

But the rules that have come out of our practice in applying the agrarian law are roughly these:

First, size: No man should own and operate privately more than a stated acreage for stated crops.

Second, production: Anyone who owns land has to use it efficiently to produce.

Third, some land is held as a cooperative and some is made into a Government-owned enterprise. The general rule here is: where there's a big investment required and not many workers needed—that's a Government-owned farm. Otherwise, those few workers, if they were a cooperative, would become millionaires. In cattle, for instance. But where there is not so much investment and more workers are needed—that's a cooperative Sugar and tobacco, for instance.

Our agrarian reform is the taking back of what's ours. The old order was a private appropriation of public property. So we've taken it back into the public domain and we're using every inch of it for the benefit of everyone now. Those are the rules and regulations of our economic revolution.

So the master key to our new economy is the agrarian reform, and maybe ours is the first agrarian reform in the world which *began* right away with an increased production. Partly, this has been due to the fact that we didn't have many little owners, but instead these big factories in the fields. So, we could start out with the efficiencies of larger scale units of production. There were no political problems about small holders. Our peasants were not each clinging to an unproductive little piece of land. They were already working on big outfits. And those that weren't, those that are individual small owners, are coming to see that it is better for them to join with one another. First, because in this way they could grow more stuff and grow it more easily, and second, as we've already said, because they saw that they could then have houses and medical centers and schools for everybody in one place, as well as the stores we've built close to where they live so they can buy the things they need.

The agrarian reform was much more difficult than, say, the nationalization of industry. You can nationalize industry in one or two days, that is no problem, but agrarian reforms are much more difficult. Every critic thought that it would all collapse right away, when we started. One very radical feature of it is that we have narrowed the old price gap between what the farmer gets for the things he grows and what the consumer pays for these things. And also the price the farmer pays for things he buys: In our people's stores, we have all the advantages of a big chain store, but these stores belong to us.

But back up a moment. Do you happen to know anything about farming? You do know, of course, that in most of Latin America, that's the biggest problem of them all. We Cubans are working out one set of answers to it; our Mexican brothers have been working out another; the Bolivians still another—the rest don't seem to be working on it at all. Now, in our new Cuban answer, Yankees are not involved at all. We Cubans, as we've told you, are in a do-it-yourself kind of movement. For example, we are not capitalists and we are not building a capitalist society in Cuba today. Neither are we building a Stalinist society. We ourselves don't know quite what to call what we are building, and we don't care. It is, of course, socialism of a sort. We're not a bit afraid of that word—and why ever should you be?

After all of us have worked so hard and for so long, after we've done all the work for generations, why should we turn over these big estates to private capitalists— Cuban or Yankee or anybody else, and allow them to keep our land? It's ours, we have it now, and we are working it.

Anyone who knows anything about farming knows that small pieces of land are not as workable as larger pieces. For one thing, to avoid toil of a very inhuman kind, you have got to have machines, and you can't use machines well on just an acre or two. You need a bigger piece of land. You need to pool your lands and your labor. And that's what we're doing in our rural cooperatives and on our Government farms.

Of course, you must realize that what you've got now in much of Latin America is not the private capitalism that your politicians talk about, but that your own farmers have long ago forgotten. What you've got in Latin America are great corporations and branches of monopolies run by managers and officials. That's not our Cuban way, not any more.

But if you don't agree with us—if you want private capitalism in poverty-stricken rural countries, if you really mean what you say about "Individual, Free, Private Enterprise," there is a way you can try to get it:

Make those huge Yankee corporations that now dominate so many areas of Latin America get out of there.

Stop supporting those generals and land owners who make themselves the only capitalists in our countries— and inefficient ones at that. And when you can help us to get rid of them, do so.

Then, help start up a real class of genuinely free farmers and small businessmen. But how? It's easy. Produce in your factories some combination agricultural tool—built around a very small tractor with different attachments to it, for plowing, for cultivating, and so on. A one-man outfit.

We don't believe such a plan would work. We believe it would be disastrous. But why don't you try it, if you really believe in free, private enterprise? It's not our Cuban way—we're not crackpots, but practical men, although it *is* genuinely free, private enterprise. So if you believe in that, do it.

In all our plans for industry we are assuming our *total* market, because in a few years if all goes well, we will certainly whip completely the problem of unemployment, and we will increase the rural standard of living to an adequate level. Our target is as much economic autonomy for Cuba as possible. That is why we are diversifying our export market and our import sources.

Just now, technical knowledge is not so important in Cuba as many foreign observers assume. We can always get technical assistance for industry, and we have Cubans ready to be trained—at first, under foreign teachers; later—sooner than you can imagine—we will train ourselves. We are already giving in INRA several short courses for administrators of agricultural and industrial concerns. For example, we have 27 students in rationalization courses alone. We now study our shoe production in terms of rationalization. In all of industry we already have some three to four hundred students. They study in the evening, while already holding those positions. In the industry department of INRA, they study accounting and administration and production, and other such things.

Most of the foreign technicians who are helping us have come from the U.N. organizations. There are many Chileans here and some Argentinians, Mexicans, and Japanese. We also have French, and German—East and West. As of now, Russian and Chinese technicians do only trade studies for possible markets. But when we get the factories from them, they will send men to teach Cubans how to operate them.

Yes, we have now bought some industrial plants from the Soviet countries. These will provide directly for employment. And they are tailored to replace the finished commodity that we had previously to import into Cuba, mainly from you. It is easier to plan our investments in such smaller plants, mainly for consumer goods now, than it is to plan for heavier industry. Heavy industrial investments are so important a choice we can't decide them so quickly, so now we study and work out the fields that it will be best for us to go into in the future, so far as heavy capital goods are concerned, keeping in mind our sources of raw materials.

IV

There is one very important point about our economic construction which you must understand—especially if you are concerned about communism and all that. We don't know how much you really know about the Soviet, or to be precise, about Stalin's way of going about industrialization. To tell you the truth, most of us don't know very much about it either, but we do know enough to realize that Stalin's old way is not our new Cuban way. Our revolutionary leaders, those in charge of our economic construction, as well as all of us, are quite plainly anti-Stalin in economic matters.

What Stalin did was to invest enormous amounts of human labor in big, heavy industry, and to do that he had to keep the production of consumer goods at very, very low levels. Also, he didn't really solve the problem of agricultural production. Now, because of this, because the people of a generation or two couldn't see the results of the policy—they couldn't eat better because of steel production—Stalin had to be politically repressive and cruel. There's no need to go into why he felt he had to do that. Stalin is dead now, and things are getting better over there in Russia. But we Cubans can certainly understand why he might have felt he had to do it. He really was alone, and he really was surrounded by hostile countries. Maybe he felt that he was in a deadly struggle, and that either he had to put the Soviet Union ahead of the capitalist world industrially, or it would crush the Soviet Union. Catch up fast or be crushed! But we don't want to argue about that. We bring it up only to make it clear to you that Stalin's economic way is not our Cuban way. It doesn't have to be:

We are not alone, as the Soviet Union then was.

We don't face the political condition Stalin faced in the countryside.

Moreover, we Cubans have a responsibility we are well aware of—to show the possibility of a new way of economic development to the Americas without sacrificing a generation or more in the making of a decent economy. We revolutionaries have dedicated ourselves to this.

And that means we have dedicated ourselves, first of all, to the agrarian reform, and second, to light industries with which we can turn out things our people can immediately use to live better with, things we can make with our own "waste products" from the crops we grow. We know that we are also going to need heavier industry. We are working on that too, but it must come a little later—although, given our resources, our trade relations with the world, and the velocity of our economic revolution, it won't be so far away as you might suppose. Next year—1961—for example, we are going to have a one-million ton steel plant. We've got the iron ore, and good manganese, of course; we'll have to get the coal from some place. By the way, you could sell it to us—will you? But never mind; if you don't, we'll get it somewhere else.

So think about our economic way like this: at one extreme—say, Stalin's old way—the agricultural problem wasn't solved and there was very little or no consumer-goods industry; everything went into big heavy industry—for the future. And there were no friends to help the Soviet Union economically.

At the other extreme—perhaps it was Peron's way in Argentina—agriculture was left in a stale condition; there was no heavy industry and no real planning for it. Practically everything went into the consumer-goods industry. Also, Peron had no friends to help him economically.

V

We don't want you to think that all this we've been telling you about is just dreaming. Our revolution is already economic construction. If you come to Cuba and look around the island, you might think that everything is pretty disorganized, or unorganized. But that's not really the case—at least not any more.

What you'd see if you drove all over Cuba would be new chicken hatcheries, and, not far from them, chicken farms where 8-week-old broilers are being raised. For the first time in the history of Cuba, the rural population is going to have plenty of good, clean chicken to eat at prices they çan afford. Who is raising these chickens? People who just yesterday were squatting in miserable, filthy *bohíos* between the highway and the cane fields. We took the younger people from their *bohíos* and trained them a little in chicken production. We built concrete block houses for these people with tile floors and toilets in them, and they helped build the long sheds of poles and straw matting for the baby chickens. Also, they've built a stand in front by the road, to sell cooked chickens to our national tourists, and in the back yard, these people are going to grow oranges.

Who's for the revolution? Those people who are now raising chickens. (By December 1960 we figure we'll have about 60 such farms, producing some 6,000,000 chickens a month; in 1961, we'll double that.)

Who's for the revolution? The people who will be eating the chickens that these people are raising. You see how it's working?

And that's the *economic* truth about our Cuban revolution: Economics aren't so complicated; all you need is the good soil and the willing people and a little equipment and organization—and the will to live decently. In Cuba, that's a revolutionary will. In Cuba, it's all being done.

But it's not just the chickens. It's also the fish. It's been known for a long time that Cuban waters are fabulously rich in fish, but nobody ever set up a real fishing industry, and the people living on this island didn't eat fish. Now we're building a fishing fleet. For the first time, we're building boats, in series production, ten at a time; in three lengths—33 feet, 50 feet, and 120 feet. We launched the first boat in January 1960. We've reduced the cost and the time it takes to build boats because we've taught the workers to work from a pattern or model, and now they say that they'll never build anything again without such patterns to work from. With our fishing cooperative, we're going to get fish to the rural people who have never had fish before. All the rural stores we've set up have refrigerators, of course, and we've already some refrigerator trucks and we're getting more. We have a freezing plant, too, for the fish. Ultimately, we'll have a frozen-food industry, of course, but for now we must depend on refrigeration. We hope —although how can we know?—to export our shrimp and oysters to the United States.

Then there is the problem of lard. It has been a big item in the Cuban diet, and we've had to import it from the United States. So that was bad both medically and economically. What we're doing about it is to raise peanuts, for the good oil in them. Peanuts are a big thing in Cuba today, and near where they are growing we are setting up the plants to process the oil from them.

We're raising cotton now, too, for the first time on any scale in Cuba. And nearby we are making thread from it. In one province we've already more than 50,000 acres in cotton, and a textile plant nearby: we got that from the Japanese.

We've already made and set up for "planting" the long, concrete trays to raise tomatoes hydraulically

(We used to import tomatoes from you!) And nearby, we've opened up a long-closed factory, to make tomato sauces and such things. We've planted tens of thousands of acres with eucalyptus trees on land that's just not been used at all. It's a wonderful tree that matures in Cuba in only ten years, and we're going to get cellulose from it as well as wood.

We're going into chemicals and paper, made from sugar-cane products. We have pilot plants to work the by-products from cane. Never before was this sort of thing done in any serious way in Cuba. Paper was the only by-product from sugar cane, yet we did not have enough paper to cover even Cuban needs. Acoustical tiles we are also making from cane by-products.

But we can't tell you about it all. You'll have to come down and see for yourself. We'd be glad to have you. And now, there are a great many motels and hotels we've built all over the island—not just the big monstrosities in Havana; they were for gamblers—for our national tourists, where you could stay too, and very reasonably. Perhaps you'd like to stay on the Isle of Pines.

The Isle of Pines is now becoming a lumber and cattle center, with some citrus fruits. Rebel soldiers have already planted 600,000 eucalyptus trees. By Christmas, they will have planted 5,000,000 of these trees, thus transforming the Isle of Pines into Eucalyptus Island! Pangola pasture is in the fields here, too: it is ready for the cattle. Pangola makes a wonderful pasture for us. It resists the terrible invasions of brush—*maarabu* (a scrub or brush we have in Cuba)—and its protein content is very high—you can run 40 head of beef cattle on each 33-acre unit of it, without any extra feeding of the cattle. And the Isle of Pines used to import its meat from Havana!

It was the center for smuggling, because it was a free port. The Batista government left it a "free port" because, of course, they were in on the smuggling and the bribery that went with it. The chief smuggler in Cuba, in the old order, was the chief of the armed forces—he was really the cover-up for his two sons, one of whom was head of the air force, the other the head of Batista's aides. They set up several stores under the name "Free Importers" to sell the stuff that was smuggled—everything from refrigerators right on up and down.

But now the Isle of Pines is becoming a new part of the new Cuba: a place of production. The big ideological fight going on in the Isle of Pines is between eucalyptus trees and pangola grass.

VI

We can't give you statistics on all we've done, because frankly, we're only now setting up a central statistical board. We've just plunged in on all fronts. Since everything was needed there wasn't much danger of our overproducing anything! And there wasn't much need of any elaborate bureaucracy to run it.

Of course, we've been a little disorganized. But why is this the case? It is less for lack of any system than because we inherited disorder. The only thing really organized in the Batista era was bribery. So of course we've been disorganized, but in our own way, every day, we are getting better organized.

We are glad to say that our revolution is less an efficient bureaucratic government than a bunch of outfits each of them working like hell at real tasks and accomplishing them. You might say that we revolutionaries in our very persons—above all, Fidel himself—embody the antibureaucracy principle! We're unsystematic—it might seem from the outside. But the revolution has its own system—it's unsystematically systematic. That is why everyone who doesn't understand our revolution is so amazed at how much we have done in so short a time. That is why they all said, and they are still saying: "It's bound to collapse in thirty days." Well, now you can see how wrong they've been. We're not amazed at what we've done. We knew we could do it. We're not going to collapse. The revolution has its own system. It goes along, and in its wake it leaves poultry houses full of chickens, and new schools—and men and women full of hope, and working hard and well.

But it is true we are now reaching the time when we can't just camp out like this much longer. The time when almost anyone could run a cooperative farm, and a lot of people suddenly began to do so, that is passing. We can't be setting up new industries in a hit-or-miss fashion. We need, and now we're beginning to get, a more orderly and centralized, a more systematic and farsighted way of doing things. Out of the actual work we're doing, we're beginning to get some rules and regulations for our new economy.

But who has been in charge of it all? Mainly INRA— our national institute of agrarian reform. We suppose INRA is a rather curious institution—to outsiders; but to us who've been through the revolution, it's the most direct and simple way to carry out the Cuban revolution.

Personnel used to be a difficult problem, but now everyone is learning so fast, it won't be a problem for long. Think what we've done in just 15 months. Many times the rebel soldiers of INRA depended more on the peasants than on the engineers. For example, in rice, the engineers said to put on four tons of fertilizer. But the peasants said no, only two tons; if you put on four, you will burn the rice. The engineers, who lacked practice, turned out to be wrong, because we tried it both ways and found out. Two tons are enough. Four tons burns the rice.

The University of Oriente and INRA work closely together now. In this respect, Oriente U. is much better than Havana U. Sixty peasants are now students at the university. INRA pays for their course and loans some teachers to the university. They are studying cotton production, and when their 13-week course is over they will be foremen. We also have courses planned in rice, in peanuts, in poultry. We're trying to reduce the prices of all these things by more efficient production. The Cuban diet needs more fruit and vegetables and salads. We also need teachers and social workers to teach the women to cook these things—how to prepare different dishes out of vegetables, for instance.

They used to say that we Latin Americans didn't know how to work, that we were just naturally lazy. But that was never true. That's another lie we Cubans have shown up. We were forced to sell our work, and our crops, at a fixed price. We knew we were being cheated, so what was the use of working?—that is what we asked ourselves. Now we see by INRA that we do get something for our work. When INRA raised the price of various commodities, to a fair price, you should have seen us go to work. And our machinery we're working 20 hours each day—the other 4 hours we use to grease and maintain it.

But again, who is "we?" Who is doing all this? Well, almost everybody is in on it in some way, but we are led in our economic construction by INRA, and of course by Fidel Castro himself. INRA and Fidel himself, they are the real movers and shakers.

INRA used to build roads, up to the end of 1959, but now most road building is in the hands of the Department of Public Works.

INRA used to build schools until last February 1960, but now the Ministry of Education is in charge of that. Also, hospitals until February 1960, but now the Department of Public Health does that. We are now planning and coordinating the work of all these departments.

It's been necessary to do things this way because INRA started in rural areas where there were no roads, and so INRA just built the roads. And in the rural cooperatives, everything comes to a point of intersection: education, roads, medical care, construction, and all the rest. But we try to keep all of this as simple as possible.

INRA is a vanguard, an economic pilot, constantly beginning new things and always leaving in its wake a variety of jobs for the various ministries to do. Is there some tricky thing to build, to set up, without any routine for building it? If that is the case, INRA will do it.

So INRA is a provisional government, but it is also a builder of government.

The economic government we are building in this way is a pragmatic outfit. But we are getting it more systematic as we go along. It is not as disorganized as it might seem to outsiders from abroad.

Our Prime Minister, Fidel, is the key to it. He plans and works and sits in on both INRA decisions and those of the Council of Ministers. He likes to persuade people; he does not like to force them. That is why he argues for hours, in order to persuade them. He wants everyone to be convinced, and he will change his own mind, if you can convince him. He is not a stubborn man.

The *commandantes* of INRA are not under the orders of any minister. Up to now, they have had to be free to go ahead. The different ministers meet very often, of course, with themselves and with others, and they are in on the planning of policy with the Prime Minister. The *commandantes* do not do this. They administer INRA. In fact, INRA is the "executive" branch of our Government. The Council of Ministers is the closest thing we have to a "legislature."

We have already got an investment schedule for each INRA zone into which our country is divided, and in time, of course, the INRA heads will be more administrative. The premium now is more and more on technical competence. Some people will fall out of the administration, if they don't acquire this competence. But, earlier, if INRA had waited for the personnel that they really "needed" to take over the Latifundia, they would not have made the agrarian reform, and then the *Latifundistas* would be undermining the Government. But the time when "everyone could run a farm" is now passing. Although, even so, you might notice that our ministers talk more about "competent personnel" than do the INRA men; the *commandantes* say, "People learn so fast, it's not much of a problem, or very soon won't be."

But the great economic fact about Cuba is that the revolution is moving on and building new Cuban institutions: agricultural cooperatives and schools and medical centers and chicken farms and tomato-sauce plants and all the rest of what is needed for a decent life. No one, we believe, could reverse this revolution—unless someone comes down here and kills a lot of Cubans. We couldn't do what had to be done in all these connections if your corporations controlled our economy. So—and it's that simple to us—we took over these corporations.

Our taking back of all these properties the foreigners

took from us, mainly the Yankee monopolies, that is now a fact that's accomplished, and it isn't going to be undone. We Cubans have worked these properties for years, for generations, and now we are going to use them to build a decent standard of life in Cuba, by Cubans, for Cubans.

So, economically as well as in every other way, we're a do-it-yourself outfit. But our do-it-yourself is not any kind of playing, like yours is. Ours is the building up of a new Cuba. It's a social and economic and military do-it-yourself. And we are going to win.

F I V E

COMMUNISM AND CUBA

We know that this is important to you—all these many questions about communism in Cuba—and we want you to know that it is important to us, too—although perhaps in a different way than to you. So let us talk about it together calmly, taking up one question at a time.

First, let us consider the questions that have to do with what your politicians call "International Communism." Are we Cuban revolutionaries under such influence? As individuals, as a ruling group, as a people? Are we being influenced by the Soviet Union? The answer is surely clear.

The answer is, "Yes, of course we are." All countries and all peoples in the world today, especially the poor ones, are under such influence. They are also under North American influence, so that's not the question, as we Cubans see it.

The real question is: What *kinds* of influence; or, better, what does it mean to say that we Cubans are under the influence of "International Communism"?

Does it mean that we are taking political and military *orders* from agents of Russia or of China, or any other country, and that we have no choice about these orders?

Or does it mean that we are voluntarily taking technical advice and economic aid from them?

If it means the first, that is one thing. But if it means the second, then there is room for free maneuvering by us, and by you too, if you want to maneuver. There *is* a world-wide competition going on, you know, and in this competition, we Cubans don't think you or your Government can avoid assuming that the advice and the aid we are taking from Russia, we are taking voluntarily.

That happens to be the plain truth. We haven't done all this fighting to get out from under one tyranny just to stick our necks into some other yoke—any other yoke. We're taking orders only from ourselves.

But even if you don't believe this, still you've got to act as if it is the case; to act as a government at all, you Yankees must act as if we Cubans are *not,* as your politicians say, "under Communist orders." Certainly, among our leaders and among our public, there are differences of opinion *and* of knowledge on this question, as on many questions. We are a political people, and each of us—as well as each of you—must work for his own beliefs within and between all these groups. That's what politics is all about, isn't it?

But again, we have to ask you: What does it mean to be under Communist influence? As for the *domestic* policies and leaders we Cubans are following—we'll talk about that later on. The point we must speak to first is "the international influence." On both these counts, we must consider the influences in economic orientation, in cultural and technical aid, in political ways of thought and action, and finally in terms of some military realities.

I

Let us begin with cultural influences and technical aid—for this is now a small but a definite part of the Cuban scene. And we hope it will become a larger part. We've already told you something about our foreign technicians. We're trying, for example, to bring some teachers, as well as other kinds of skilled people, from Mexico to Cuba. Twenty-five years ago, the Spanish intellectual elite, exiles from that war, passed through Cuba on the way to Mexico, and now we are trying to get them to come back here. And we've already gotten economic experts and other qualified people from Chile and elsewhere in Latin America, as well as Europe East and West. Yes, there *are* Russians and Chinese, Polish and Czech people among us, and we are very glad to welcome them. Right now there are not very many but when we get some factories from these countries, we hope there will be many technicians from there to show

us how to run the machinery. And we're going to welcome them.

Let us say at once we'd be glad if you too would send
us such people as they are sending. But you've not done
that. What engineers, sanitation experts, ballet companies, irrigation technicians, agricultural exhibitions,
symphony orchestras, oil experts, exhibitions of painting,
soil analysts—what has the U.S. Government arranged for
and sent to our revolutionary Cuba?

The answer is None. What you sent that we certainly
do remember were the Military Missions—to Batista;
they helped train his soldiers to kill us. Those are the
technicians you sent. They became a horrible part of the
everyday life of Cuba, and you did not withdraw these
Pentagon missions until it was obvious to everyone in
the world, even to the people in your Pentagon, that Batista was through.

But nowadays, *no* military missions from anywhere are
with us. We know very well how to fight, if we must, and
we do not need military missions, yours or anyone else's.
What we do need and what we are getting is the assistance of technicians.

Take our economic relations next. The Soviet Union
and other Communist countries are buying our sugar
and selling us oil as well as other things we need. We
are doing business with them. It's a good economic deal
—for us, at least, and we think for them too. You know
"a good business deal" when you see one, don't you,
Yankee? Your corporations that have dominated Cuba's
economy, they certainly know! But we've already told
you about *their* economic relations with the old Cuba.
Do the Russians have that kind of exploitative relations with the Cuban economy today? They certainly
do not. And as long as they don't, we're going to keep
on doing business with them.

It just happens that the Soviet bloc and the underdeveloped countries have many opportunities—in plain
economic terms—to benefit mutually from economic
traffic. As their own standards go up, these Soviet
countries need more raw materials of the sort we in
Latin America are producing. It's not merely a gift

we're getting from them. We're doing economic business together. We'll do it with you too, or anybody else, if it works out fairly to our mutual economic benefit. If you don't believe it, try us and see.

As for our "recognition" of China, as well as our Chinese trade, the only thing we need to say is this: If your Government is so foolish as to think they can accomplish *anything* by not "recognizing" over 600 million people, we Cubans are not. We are not ostriches. We want news about China. We want to do business with China. They are very much a part of the world we all live in, and we want to live in it with them, not try to act as if they didn't exist. Besides, it's none of your Government's business what countries our Government recognizes, is it? It's none of our business, but still we'll say it: What you ought to do is pull your Government's head out of the mud and make it recognize the fact of China, too.

But getting to what we suppose is your main worry —take communism as a military problem. We Cubans don't think this is nearly as important, at least now, as your Yankee politicians seem to.

Has the Soviet Union set up a base on Cuban soil? No.

But the United States has a naval base in Cuba.

But, you may say, Cuba's so close to the United States—that had to be?

But you also have bases all around the perimeter of the Soviet bloc, as close as you can possibly get them.

So if we *did* allow the Soviet Union to build and to maintain a base in Cuba—and unless your Government forces us to, we are not going to do that—you would have no moral claim, no political right, to object. You have bases in Turkey, a few miles from the Soviet border, and in Japan, on Okinawa, on Taiwan—all of them, and others, just a little distance from the borders of China. If you do not see the point, please know that we do. So do most of the peoples of the world. And very soon —please do not doubt it—more of them will.

Moreover, just ask yourself this question: Why should

the Russians *want* a military base here in Cuba? They believe bases are obsolete. Their rockets go much further than the 90 miles that separates our island from your continent, and besides, it seems to us, the Russians want to carry on their great contest with you by *non*-military means. Surely that is becoming clear to you. Culturally, economically, politically—that is the way they want to fight you, and we are all for that. Any fool in Cuba knows this is the only sane way to carry on the world contest, although wise men in your country often do not seem to.

But no matter how all that may seem to you, we Cubans are not going to allow the Russians, or anyone else, to build any base here; not unless—we must repeat it—your Government forces us to. We do not like foreign bases. We do not like generals, either—yours or ours, or anybody else's.

Anyway, don't you see that it's not the military issue that is crucial now—unless you attack us. Men take up arms only when politics fails; it's in political terms that the technological aid and the economic traffic, *and* the military issues, must be worked out between civilized men.

But the· major politics between *us* has been the Monroe Doctrine. And it is true that we Cubans *are* challenging that doctrine, as we understand it and as your Government and corporations have used it—which is only to say: We are going to be an independent nation with a sovereign state.

For what does the national freedom of a sovereign state mean if it does not mean that it has control in its own territory, over its own resources, over its own military force? Well, have we Cubans been free in these respects? Obviously we have not been. Are we Cubans now so free? Obviously, that is our big international objective.

President Monroe was your President about 137 years ago. That is a long time; what he said is not exactly eternal. He was not a Cuban, anyway, nor a Brazilian, a Mexican, a Chilian. He was a Yankee. And this Monroe Doctrine with all the things that have been added to it and the interpretations made of it, these are not doctrines built on any consultation with any of the governments of any of the peoples of Latin America. It has been a Yankee policy, enforced militarily by the United States Marines, used economically by the United States corporations, and used politically by the United States Government—to interfere in the internal and international affairs of Latin American countries.

At first—it's true—the Monroe Doctrine was just a warning to European countries to stay out of the Western Hemisphere. But then it was interpreted and reinterpreted into a justification for Yankees to dominate Latin America. In Chicago, on 2 April 1903, your President Theodore Roosevelt said:

"I believe in the Monroe Doctrine with all my heart and soul. . . . There is a homely old adage which runs: 'Speak softly and carry a big stick; you will go far.' If the American nation will speak softly and yet build and keep at a pitch of the highest training a thoroughly efficient navy, the Monroe Doctrine will go far."

Isn't that plain enough? If not, then read "Olney's Fiat." Richard Olney was your Secretary of State, and in 1895 he said:

"Today the United States is practically sovereign on this continent, and its fiat is law upon the subjects to which it confines its interposition. Why? It is not because of the pure friendship or good will felt for it. It is not simply by reason of its high character as a civilized state, nor because wisdom and justice and equity are the inevitable characteristics of the dealings of the United States. It is because, in addition to all other grounds, its infinite resources combined with its isolated position render it master of the situation and practically invulnerable as against any or all other powers. . . ."

It didn't take Mr. Khrushchev to tell us Latin Americans that the Monroe Doctrine was an outworn piece of arrogance. We know all its "interpretations" and "corollaries." We know about "the Good Neighbor policy" too, and "the Inter-American system," as well. But it's the Monroe Doctrine—as your politicians have unilaterally interpreted it—that's been your real policy and still is. This Monroe Doctrine, of course, is against the whole *idea* of the Inter-American system, although not against how that system seems to *work*. Do you know how the Monroe Doctrine—with all its official interpretations—reads today in Spanish? It reads "Yankee Imperialism," and maybe "The Marines Are Coming."

And today, it's surely a very dangerous argument for you to use. For if the United States can have a Monroe Doctrine, why then, can't the Russians and the Chinese? Your leading newspaper said, on the 25th of July 1960, that you were "the natural customers and the natural friends of the Cuban people, and they of us." But if that is so, then are not the Taiwanese and the Japanese the "natural customers" and so on of China? And are not Turkey and Afghanistan the "natural friends" of Russia? Well, if that is not so—what *is* the difference?

Please don't tell *us* that *they* are tyrannies and that you Yankees are all for freedom everywhere, and that this is the difference. We know something about your freedom, for other peoples—we've lived *under* it.

II

A few of us, who have had time to think about such big problems, have wanted Cuba to be neutral, like India. Of course, not everyone in Cuba agrees with us. There are differences among us about all such big issues, but you haven't helped us to think clearly about them. Sometimes, these days, we feel that you are *forcing* us to say *"Cuba, sí! Yankee, no!"* and just not mention Russia at all.

One of the many ways you are *not* helping us is this curious idea you seem to have of how history is being made. You always seem to think that those tens of millions of people who are rising up against you (eight million people, we have read, took part in the demonstrations against you in Japan recently), that they are just somehow misguided—and absolutely controlled by small conspiratorial groups of trouble-makers, under direct orders from Moscow and Peking. You must think that they are diabolically omnipotent if you think that it is *they* who *create* all this messy unrest for you, that it is *they* who have given tens of millions the idea that they shouldn't want to remain or to become the seat of American nuclear bases—those gay little outposts of North American civilization we've read about in your magazines.

But you are wrong, Yankee—very wrong. It's you who are being misguided by your own propaganda. Those people don't want your U-2's on their territories. They want to get out of the American military machine. They don't want to be tangled up among you crazy big antagonists. They don't want their societies to be made military garrisons. And in all this we must say we agree with them.

But on the other hand, it's more complicated than that. First of all, it's a fact that we *are* in a cold war with *you,* which, as we've already told you, we fear your Government may turn into a hot war. And in this war between Yankees and Cubans, the Russians and the Chinese and the others who are with them, they have helped us and they are helping us. Ours is the war we care about, and we are very grateful to them for offering to help us in it. So how can we really be neutral about your big cold war with them?

At first, you must remember, it wasn't like this at all. Back in August 1959—which in our revolutionary time is a very long time ago—our Minister of Foreign Affairs said very clearly to the world that we Cubans were trying "to hold our own unmistakable position." At the conference at Santiago, Chile, he said out loud that "the Cuban revolution is neither to the right nor to the left of anyone." He meant it is ahead of them both! Then he quoted our Prime Minister, Fidel Castro, who a little earlier had said:

"Standing between the two political and economic ideologies or positions being debated in the world, we are holding our own position. We have named it humanism, because its methods are humanistic, because we want to rid man of all fears, directives, or dogmatisms. We are revolutionizing society without binding or terrorizing it. The tremendous problem faced by the world is that it has been placed in a position where it must choose between capitalism, which starves people, and communism, which resolves economic problems but suppresses the liberties so greatly cherished by man. Both Cubans and Latin Americans cherish and foster a revolution that may meet their material needs without sacrificing those liberties. Should we accomplish this by democratic means, the Cuban revolution will become a classic example in the history of the world.

"Our idea of freedom is different from that of the reactionaries who talk of elections but not of social justice. Without social justice, democracy is not possible, for without it men would be slaves of poverty. That is why we have said that we are one step ahead of the right and of the left, and that this is a humanistic revolution, because it does not deprive man of his essence, but holds him as its basic aim. Capitalism sacrifices man; the Communist state, by its totalitarian concept, sacrifices the rights of man. That is why we do not agree with any of them. Each people must develop its own political organization, out of its own needs, not forced upon them or copied; and ours is an autonomous Cuban revolution. It is as Cuban as our music. Can we conceive of all peoples listening to the same music? Such is the reason for my saying that this revolution is not red, but olive-green, for olive-green is precisely our color, the color of the revolution brought by the rebel army from the heart of the Sierra Maestra."

That wasn't, and that isn't, "mere rhetoric." It seems pretty clear to us: our revolutionary Government tried very hard to be "neutral," to stay on its own, to work out its own destiny with all nations that would help us, regardless of whether they were red or red-white-and-blue. We tried to be explicitly olive-green.

But the truth is—and you must know it now after all we've told you—your Government hasn't let us be just olive-green. By what they've done politically and economically against us, and by what they failed to do, your imperialists and politicians have been forcing us to establish economic and political relations with "the other side," and also to be grateful to them because they really have helped us. By its military threat to us, your Government has forced us to be very grateful to the Russians for their offer of military aid, should it be necessary, against you.

Don't you see that? It's the plain truth of the matter. And if you think it's not the whole truth, well then, you tell us the rest of it, will you, please?

In the meantime, the way things have developed, under pressure from your Government mainly, we can't now proclaim any neutralism—as we tried to do, a year or so ago. We can't and we don't want to, because it would be a false sentiment. We Cuban revolutionaries have faced immediate facts as we have come up against them. We've been forced to react to this fact, and then to that fact, as we've gone along our revolutionary road. We're a pilot state and an experimental nation. Most of us have never even thought about communism or capitalism or about your cold war with the Russians, until we got involved in it in the course of our own Cuban revolution. And what we *know* about the Soviet Union and about the United States is what we've experienced with each of you. And that experience has led to this:

We see the United States in terms of what we've suffered at the hands of your Government and your monopolies and the Yankee Marines; we see you as materialism without any philosophy, and closed off by yourselves in your own selfish interests.

We see the Soviet Union in terms of their very decisive economic traffic with us, and their offer to help us if you attack us militarily. We are afraid of that attack, and so we are glad of their offer. And in terms of these experiences with the Soviet Union, which you cannot deny without lying, what do you expect us to think about them? We are beginning to think that the Soviet peoples are perhaps a materialistic people with a philosophy. We don't know much about that philosophy, but it does seem to us that they believe in science and industry to help people and not to exploit them. So far at least, that has been *our* experience with them.

But it is not a question of philosophy; it is a question first of economic and political interests, and then of the ideologies that serve them. We think that what gives its character to our revolution is the fight between North America and Latin America. That's *our* cold war. And if the Soviet Union helps us in constructive, bold, decisive ways, and you keep trying to hurt us in destructive ways, how then could you expect us to be "neutral," much less to be for you?

Maybe we shouldn't put all this so candidly, but why not? We've nothing to hide, and we are not afraid of you any longer. There are many influences and forces between the two extremes which the Russians and the Yankees take. But then, surely you are beginning to realize that your attitudes toward *them* are rather extremist in the world today, and getting to be more and more unique, too. So, here's how many of us in Cuba see it:

Suppose you had not cut our sugar quota. Suppose that you had sold us oil. Suppose you had not supported Batista. Suppose you had sent technicians to Cuba, instead of Military Missions to Batista. Suppose you hadn't tried to stop West European countries from selling us farm machinery, arms, and giving us credit. Suppose you had helped us, instead of trying to hamper us—then do you think we should have needed to go to Russia for help?

Our Prime Minister went to Washington, right away after the insurrection, but he was just given the cold shoulder, and certainly no help. Even his request for quite minor financial consideration was turned down flat.

Certainly we'd still have had differences about payments to U.S. corporations for example, and other things, too; but all those could have been negotiated fairly. We could have settled them with honor to all of us—if only your Government had really wanted to, had really tried to, and had known how to go about controlling the Yankee vested interests rather than being controlled by them.

But they did not want to. Anyway, they did not try. Maybe they just did not know how.

Instead, they tried to stop our revolution, once it really got under way, in the economic and social ways in the countryside that *we* wanted it to go on. And that is the real key to it all, Yankee:

You simply do not understand what we are about.

You simply do not understand what must be done in revolutionary countries like Cuba.

You have no way to respond to it, except in the crazy, panic ways you do. They *are* crazy ways: they do not, as you must see now, accomplish whatever you've wanted to accomplish.

But the Communist nations *do* know how to respond: they do help us. We know that it may be a perilous thing for us to accept their help, but as you often say, yet never seem to realize: It's dangerous all over.

And what, we must ask you, has been our alternative—to let you starve out our revolution, to let your corporations continue to dominate our economy, to let you keep us a hungry colony of yours—you, already the richest country in the world? As you must know, our answer is: *"Cuba, sí! Yankee no!"*

That answer does not necessarily mean, "Russia, yes"—unless you force it to mean that.

Externally, we do not want to be dependent on anyone, Communist or capitalist, or anybody else. We want to be an independent nation, deciding as a nation what our international policies are going to be. We have not fought and died to become the lackeys of Communists or of capitalists or of anybody else.

Internally, we do not want to be enslaved by any dictatorship to the left, to the right, or in the middle. We've had all the tyranny we want, and now we want to be a free people, deciding as a people how we're going to live our lives. And that's what we are doing now.

In the meantime, let us tell you a little joke we Cubans don't always think is altogether a joke. When Mikoyan went back to Moscow, Khrushchev asked him: "Why are you looking so worried?" And Mikoyan answered: "These Cubans have infiltrated that damned Communist Party of Cuba!" And it wasn't very long until everyone in Moscow just knew that Mikoyan, after all, was a Cuban agent.

Here's another story: It is said, although we don't know, that the following actually happened. Anyway, it certainly sounds like Fidel. In August 1960, in Pinar del Rio, in one of the new motels the revolutionary Government has built for national tourism, the new Soviet Ambassador to Cuba first met our Prime Minister. It was an accidental meeting; the Prime Minister was working, as usual; the Soviet Ambassador was touring the country to get acquainted with some of our problems. His Spanish is fluent. He was in his shirtsleeves without any tie, something we're sure Fidel noticed and liked. The conversation went like this:

The Soviet Ambassador said: "The peoples of the Soviet Union express their admiration of the courage of the Cuban people, and wish. . . ."

"Thank you very much, sir," Fidel interrupted. "Now, Mr. Ambassador, by next Christmas we need three thousand tractors. We've got plenty of bulldozers so don't worry about that. But we could really use those tractors."

The Soviet Ambassador said: "Perhaps our specialists could discuss the specifications of. . . ."

Fidel: "Yes, of course, now we need three types. Two hundred of them should be, etc., etc., etc. . . . And by the way, why don't you Russians quit planting all those damned sugar beets. We've got plenty of sugar! You plant corn! I understand you can raise *magnificent* corn over there, this high! And look, Mr. Ambassador, how about those boats you've got that go on skis? How fast do they go? How many people do they carry? Are they for quiet waters only? Really? Over 200 people? Are you sure? We need a couple of those. And listen, if you run into any trouble and can't get those 3,000 tractors for us by Christmas, you let me know, will you? I'll go over there and talk to those Russian workers! They can produce them by Christmas, that's plenty of time."

Perhaps it wasn't exactly like that, we weren't there, but knowing our Fidel, we're sure it did go something like that. His language, most of the time, is the language of production. He is really curious about all such things. In him you see what it means to say: Revolution is construction.

III

Our Fidel Castro's no Communist, and never has been; even the Deputy Director of your own Central In-

telligence Agency—General C. P. Cabell—knows that;
he said it on 5 November 1959 to your Senate Internal
Security Subcommittee. He said that the Communists
in Cuba don't consider Fidel a Communist "or even a
pro-Communist." And that they "were unable to gain
public recognition of commitments from him during the
course of the revolution." That part he got right. Then
he said: "Within the 26th of July Movement there is
considerable evidence of opposition to communism."
Well, that's true, too. But please know this well:

Our Cuban opposition to "communism" doesn't mean
the kind of McCarthyism that you've put up with in your
country. That kind of hysterical anticommunism is very
much the kind that prevails among your top Government people today, and they are trying very hard to
make it come about in our country, and other countries all over the world. But we're not having any of
that panic and ignorance in Cuba.

Let us put the whole business to you like this:

In our Cuba there are Communist influences—and
Yankee influences. Generally, in the past, the Yankee
influences have been counterrevolutionary—certainly
they are that today. Now, you Yankees and the Russians
are at cold war. Therefore, you must understand why we
Cubans say: Anticommunism is counterrevolutionary.
Indeed, much of it is just that. Maybe it didn't have to
be, but now it is.

We know that is not all there is to it. Would to God
it were that simple. We know we're not in the black-
or-white days. But because of your hysteria: anticommunism in Cuba is counterrevolutionary.

But what exactly *is* "communism"? There are many
roads to many different kinds of decent societies,
Marxian and non-Marxian and in between, and we are
trying very hard to stick to the idea and to the practice
of the Cuban people working out our own Cuban road.

That is much more difficult than following *any* already established road—fascist, capitalist, communist,
or whatever: It needs much more imagination, and it
is often much more perilous, especially for the leaders.

But we think we've already shown imagination and

the sense of historic daring in the making of our revolution. Now the tasks are more difficult, and sometimes more tedious for men like us. But when we find them tedious, we remember that this too is part of history we're fooling with; that this is still The Cuban Revolution we're trying to clarify and push further and make even more real in the life of the people. It's another kind of history, another phase of the revolution; and now it's far more important than the black-or-white days. For, it could, all of it, go to hell. Don't you think we know that?

"Anti-Yankeeism" is not merely some emotion we've whipped up. We hope by now we've shown you that it is due to justified grievances against U.S. imperialists and the actions of the U.S. Government—in the past and in the present. But, you may ask, to what extent is this anti-Yankeeism necessary for inside Cuba? To what extent is it a necessary basis, even if a temporary one, of our continued revolutionary enthusiasm in support of our Government? Well, we don't really know—it's mixed up, of course, with that. But if anti-Yankeeism is serving this purpose, we are trying to control it. Not because it is anti-*Yankeeism,* but because we don't really believe in such wholesale hate. It cannot be a good thing, we think to ourselves, to base a movement, a nation, a policy, a government on general hate of another people. When we say "Yankee, no!" we don't mean by "Yankee" all the people of North America. We are not such fools. If some of our people do seem to mean that—although certainly they'd never display it towards any individual from the United States—you certainly ought to be able to understand that. Still, we revolutionaries are against it, because that would be like some of *your* people—especially your top people and officials—when they shout "Communist!" Well, isn't it?

When our people shout: *"Cuba, sí! Yankee, no!"*—we know they should add after that "no" specific *kinds* of "Yankee": monopolies, officials, or whatever. For we know it's a simple-minded mistake to think that the people of any nation are all alike, and so subject to wholesale hate, or love, or any other emotion or judgment. When people hate people—Yankees or Russians or Germans—or Cubans, that's the most stupid form of nationalism, no matter what "good" might be done in its name. It is perilous for everyone. It is no way for a man to act.

So we do want to be as specific in our humanism as we can. It would be great if we Cubans could shout: *Cuba, sí! Yankee, sí! Russia, sí!* Down with counter-revolutionaries! Down with imperialists! Down with commissars!

But—you won't let us.

IV

But what about the Communist *Party* of Cuba and its influence here?

The first thing you must realize is that this Communist Party of Cuba has never been very large or very strong as a party. Your CIA deputy, at the end of 1959, estimated 17,000 Communist Party members in Cuba. Maybe so. It sounds about right.

The second thing that's important is that this party did not play any part at all in the making of our revolution. The revolution, as we've told you, was made in the Sierra Maestra, and it is there that we really won out over the tyranny. For over five years, in fact—before we won—the Communists, when they didn't ignore us, were political rivals of our movement. We owed them nothing when we triumphed over Batista's tyranny. They didn't help. And any part Communists now have in our revolutionary Government is because our Government gave them that part. They are there because they are now, like almost everyone else, helping our revolution. They didn't make any revolution.

The third thing is that the Communist Party of Cuba has been and is made up of some older intellectuals and some very poor people. It got such strength as it ever had first from the facts of exploitation—and now that is over; and second, from being a kind of symbol for young intellectuals to join—and now that's over, too.

To understand why this is so, you must realize the

fourth important thing: we Cuban revolutionaries of the 26th of July Movement are much more advanced than the Communist Party ever was or is today. Every week, some Cuban Communist or other tells us that they never dreamed we could go so far so fast—in overthrowing the tyrant, in industrializing, in the land reform, and all the rest of our revolution.

The plain fact is, our revolution has outdone the Communists on every score. From the beginning up till today, always at every turn of event and policy, the revolution is always faster than the Cuban Communist Party, or individual Communists. In all objective facts, then, we are much more radical, much more revolutionary than they. And that is why we *are* using them, rather than the reverse; they are not using us. In fact they are being very grateful to us for letting them in on the work of the revolution.

In fact, this is the case generally with local Communist parties in Latin America. In a real revolution today, in Latin America at least, the local Communists are to the right of the revolution. Here in Cuba, certainly the revolution has outpaced them and does on every front. They always arrive too late and with too little. This has been the case in Cuba and it still is the case: they lag behind our revolution.

The Communist parties in Latin America generally go for "popular fronts," and "national democratic coalitions," and so on. They haven't got sufficient popular support to make a revolution, and so they sacrifice immediate revolutionary action—and even thought—for "national movements of liberation." They are small everywhere, although sometimes rather well organized. But they are not really very well adapted for Latin American conditions of revolution. They are too much like some "Society of Friends of the Soviet Union," and they won't even go into "the China question" when you raise it; and the Chinese in Latin America, they don't fool around at all with the Communist parties here. They go directly to the left-wing element!

Many of the brilliant students in Latin America do go *through* the Communist Party, although we Cuban revolutionaries happen not to have done that. The Latin American Communist parties do have a generally high average, for Latin America; nonetheless, in all the countries here, there are brighter men outside the Communist Party than in it. Anyway, in Cuba the Communist Party men try to hold back Fidel. They say to him, "Take it easy!" But he does not pay any attention, he does not take it easy. With him at its head, the revolution is always moving along. The Communist party, and individual Communists, follow in his wake. What else can they do? But they do not now lead, and they have not led at any time in the past.

The Communist Party of Cuba is a *more or less* disciplined political organization. So, some people believe that since there *is* a lack of adequately trained administrative personnel for all the work of the revolution, the Communist Party will increase in its power, that the Communists will move into the administrative vacuum, so to speak. Maybe there's something to this. But on the other hand, consider the following:

The Cuban Communist Party is a "less" disciplined outfit than you might think. There is no evidence that the Communists in Cuba are so diabolically competent. In the first place, it's very easy for anyone who wants to join the Party to do so. But to join doesn't mean anything much. Under the tyranny, perhaps it did: It was a symbol of rebellion for a young man to join. But it isn't now such a symbol at all. What's new and real and immediate is the revolution itself and the new institutions the revolution is creating so rapidly. Young men go directly into these institutions. They've no need to join the Communists. It's the others, the more old-fashioned kind of "radical," who tend to stay with the Communist Party.

So the revolution is creating very rapidly its own "cadres." It doesn't have to lean on such apparatus as the Communist Party may have. We Cubans have a tremendous capacity to work, and even to organize things well. Certainly, we've already shown that. Moreover, those who do belong to the Communist Party of Cuba think "Cuba first, the party second." The most valuable and talented persons who happen to be Communists think in this way. Their allegiance is to the Cuban revolution, not to any abstract "communism" as such.

The truth is the Communists as a political party have very little importance in Cuba; it is only in the Yankee imagination that it is important. This party decides nothing political in or about Cuba. And we don't think that it will. There's no exploitation any more. It can't feed on that. It's no symbol of rebellion or revolution anymore. It can't feed on that.

V

Of course, there *are* three things that might increase the political power of the Cuban Communists as a party:

First, if every day in the United States the Yankees shout against "The Communists," and name them, and accuse them of being against the Yankees, then some real revolutionaries might decide to join the Communist Party! We are not just making a joke. All that anti-Cuban publicity, taking the form of anticommunism, would be an important factor in increasing the prestige, and perhaps in time, the power of individual Communists, if not of the Party, in Cuba.

Second, if the revolutionary Government of Cuba were to condemn and persecute the Communist Party—that would tend to increase the party's power as a symbol again. Then it would mean something to dare to join the party. As of now, such a symbol is 30 years out of date in Cuba.

Third, and this is certainly more serious, the power of the Communist Party might be increased if the U. S. succeeded in making serious economic difficulties for Cuba that the revolution couldn't cope with, or organized the counterrevolutionaries abroad, and with them or without them, stepped up the threats of military action against us, *and did all this in the name of anticommunism* —well, *then,* perhaps the Communist Party would gain strength, although we can't know how much. Still, maybe you'll want to think about the point. It's quite a solid point.

But for now, the overwhelming fact we think you ought to bear in mind is that our revolution is faster, deeper, and stronger than anything the Communist Party can accomplish today or tomorrow.

As we write this to you, it occurs to us that you may be thinking: "Well, maybe all that's so, about the actual Communist Party in Cuba. But so what? Your revolution itself, isn't it, after all, 'Communist'?"

Our answer is that the question is a matter of what words you want to use. We don't care what words you use. We're trying to tell you as frankly and as honestly as we can what it's actually like in Cuba today and what we're actually doing. If you want to call it "communist," well, that's okay with us. We don't really care if you are too lazy to study the varieties of left-wing governments and movements in the world today.

On the other hand, if you're seriously interested, we can tell you this: Insofar as we are Marxist or leftist (or communist, if you will) in our revolutionary development and thought, it is not due to any prior commitment to any ideology. It is because of our own development. That is true in general and it is true in detail. For example, we Cuban revolutionaries read Mao Tse-tung on guerrilla warfare after we'd been in the hills—and *then* we knew that the military and economic way of our insurrection against Batista had many similarities to Mao Tse-tung's fight in China.

And we've already told you about our anti-Stalin economic pattern.

Just now we are beginning to look into the whole variety of Marxist developments; there's not just one, you know. And they do interest some of us greatly. We're interested in all kinds of ideas for constructing our Cuban society.

We're making a revolution to solve the problems of the Cuban people. If our way of solving them, at this point or at that point, turns out to be similar to the solutions of other peoples—*any* peoples in the world—we certainly don't care.

We're practical men, not theorists—although some of us are getting more and more interested in theories, and when we've the time, we're studying them now. Send us a few practical theories, Yankees: we'll study them. But do you *have* any such theories? We've not got time for crackpot stuff, you know, but if you've any workable ideas for people like us—send them along. We'll study them.

VI

There's one final thing about "communism," or rather, more generally, "totalitarianism," that we'd like to bring up. We have nothing to hide. Most of us Cubans are not yet worrying about it; we're too busy with our revolution. But some of us know that a little later on it could become a real problem. It can be a problem for any people—you, for instance, Yankee.

It's nothing directly to do with "International Communist" influences, much less orders from abroad. And it's not due to any role of the Cuban Communist Party, much less any increase of their power. It's what you might call the totalitarian mentality and way of doing things.

Even though you are not under communist influence in any way, certainly not by any foreign apparatus, nevertheless this mentality may come about whenever there is generally a lack of culture and knowledge and education, and along with that a deadly fear of foreign menace. Because if you're in that kind of condition, then you're forced to think in black-or-white ways, and you feel the panic to make sure of the loyalties of everybody. You come to feel that you've got to *know*, then that you must insure that you know—and that *could* mean, we suppose, a hardening up of everything—even a reign of revolutionary terror.

All this is really part of the problem of a political system for Cuba. We're not worried about it just now. But some of us do think about it, when we've the time from our work to do so. Couldn't you think about it a little? If you do, please bear in mind the conditions we've

just suggested. Don't you see how *extremist* your involve-
ment with the course of our revolution has been, and is,
and is going to be?

So what does the business of Communist influence on
Cuba and in Cuba boil down to?

That you don't know and that you can't know the
exact extent and the character of such influence. Neither
do many of us. But for *you,* that is not the main point
at issue. No matter what you may believe about communism, there is only one way you can counter it. You
must begin really to compete with that influence in
positive, constructive ways. And that can only mean in
technical and cultural and economic and political ways.
If you really tried, perhaps you might win.

Or don't you think you've got a chance?

The cost of such efforts would be as nothing to the
tremendous results for the United States. throughout
Latin America alone, not to speak of the rest of the
world, which—never forget it, Yankee—is watching what
you do and what you fail to do in Cuba.

But even if you didn't "win"—whatever that may
mean to you—would not everyone in the world benefit
from such competition itself? Well, so that is what we
are thinking about communism and Cuba these days.

S I X

REVOLUTIONARY EUPHORIA

What's it like in Cuba today? Any honest man must ask himself that, as he hears and reads so many contradictory stories. The only way to know is to find out for yourself, and that is not possible for everyone, for it means that you'd have to come to Cuba and stay here for a long time. That's why we are trying to tell you what it's like in Cuba today.

Today in Cuba there's the enormous feeling of new beginnings and the ending of old evils. There's some fear, too, that new evils may arise—but then, nowadays, who hasn't such fears? We Cubans, we Latin Americans everywhere, we are all living at various points in a kind of balance; we've broken away from the old, and we don't know exactly where we're going to end up—but then, who can really know that today?

Among us there are many desperate hopes. But here's the real news from Cuba: Our hopes are already coming true. So, already in Cuba there is the hope that is based upon achievements already made and being lived in.

No one can show you any photographs of Cuba's future. Only present scenes that might become more general. We're trying to make them so: and that's what it's like in Cuba today.

I

Everyone has daydreams, but for most people these dreams are never related to their everyday life. By our revolution, we Cubans have made The Big Connection, between fantasy and reality, and now we are living in it. To us, to live in this connection, that is the fact of our revolution.

So if we try to do too much all at once, if we are at times childish, if we make terrible mistakes, if we get carried away—understand all this, Yankee, as part of an extraordinary effort. Understand all this as part of making the connection for the very first time in our lives between our daydreams and our realities.

And if you find this somehow "unwholesome," think also how unwholesome it is *never* to make the connection, but to live badly forever and yet to dream always of how it might be. Does not all glory have a touch of insanity about it? Isn't that the peril, one of them at least, of trying to make The Big Connection? For, in every revolution, that is what you must do. You must act as if you'd already made it. And that is what we Cubans are doing. We have to cling to our revolution, to all of it, the good and the bad, because now its agencies and its leaders are the means of our hopes, but more than that, of our very sanity.

From Fidel we have learned, every day we are learning, that you can go very far, if only you try hard enough. The will to see further and to see it all in big terms—what is the Yankee expression?—"to fly high." Maybe that is utopian, but that *is* what Fidel has taught us and is teaching us all the time. To dream and to believe you can make the dream come true.

The revolution is a way of defining reality.

The revolution is a way of changing reality—and so of changing the definitions of it.

The revolution in Cuba is a great moment of truth.

II

It is a moment of *military* truth. That truth is that guerrilla bands, led by determined men, with peasants alongside them, and a mountain nearby, can defeat organized battalions of the tyrants equipped with everything up to the atom bomb. About the atom bomb we don't know. Everyone thought the days of the guerrilla were over. In our moment of Cuban truth, they are seeing that they are not over.

That is not the only military truth of the Cuban revolution. We may not yet be through with the fighting. You may attack us. But in the meantime, we are proving that a revolution in a Latin American country that is against Yankee imperialism can win. People had given up that hope. We are proving, so far, that it can be a fact.

III

The revolution in Cuba is a moment of *economic* truth. It is in revolutions like ours that such truth appears, and it is then that everybody can see it. Not just the leaders, not just the intellectuals, but the ordinary men and women who never thought about such things before but only lived them. The economic truth is this:

Things economic are not so very complicated. Those who say they are, say it to keep others from knowing how easy it can be to produce and to distribute the things men need. How quickly men and women can all learn to make these things, to grow these things, for themselves! You can be good at anything if you've the will to do it. In our Cuba today, young people are no longer told: "Maybe that would be fine, but it's just not practical; this won't work; too much is against that; leave well enough alone; take it easy, now; don't get excited; buckle down; walk lightly, boy, things are not so simple." In short: Be afraid.

The economic truth of the revolution in Cuba is that you do not have to be afraid. Every day the revolution we are making is teaching us how to build a civilized, sensible economic system. You name it what you wish. We're too busy building it, and that's why just now above all else, for us: Revolution is construction.

IV

The revolution in Cuba is a moment of *political* truth, and here are the main political truths of it:

Under a tyranny, all politics of any consequence are the politics of the guerrilla.

Under conditions of poverty, all politics of any consequence are the politics of economic construction.

Under conditions of ignorance, all politics of any consequence are the politics of educational construction.

By the military and then by the economic and the educational effort, we Cubans have thrown away politics as we've known them, and also the kind of politics that you know. These don't exist in Cuba.

First, in the military moment, and then in the economic and the educational moment, all politics become irrelevant and everything becomes political. That is the political truth about Cuba today, and it is not a paradox. For the old politics we've done away with were the politics of the thief and the exploiter; the new "politics" we're in the middle of are the politics of the revolutionary who is constructing a new society. And what our future politics may turn out to be, we simply do not know.

But for now everyone who is half honest is in agreement on two general points: Before the triumph of the revolution, Cuba was a land of grief and fear and frequent horror. Under the revolutionary Government and with it we people of Cuba are enormously happy. There is no other word for it. No one dreamed, not really, that there could be such a close agreement between the felt needs of the people and men having such great power as our revolutionary leaders do have. No one dreamed that such power would not immediately corrupt men.

It is not so much that we are *re*building Cuban society, for there was nothing here of much worth to rebuild. We are *building* a new society, from top to bottom, and in all the spheres of our lives. It is the birth of a nation we are living through.

Starting with the few ill-equipped rebel soldiers, we defeated Batista's large and well-equipped battalions. Now we are building around these rebels a new type of army and citizen's militia.

Starting with thousands of acres of land—in the old order, allowed to go to weed and brush—as well as the old Latifundia and other properties stolen from us, now we are building a brand-new economic system.

Starting with illiteracy and a dreadful lack of education on all levels, we are building a completely new educational system, from kindergarten to university.

Those are the three areas in which our revolutionary Government now works all day and half the night. And, make no mistake about it: we Cubans are working with them, willingly, enthusiastically. We are full of hope and the only real worry, the only real fear we have is the menace of the United States to all our efforts.

We are not just setting up some new rulers over us. We're working out a brand-new social and economic order in Cuba. To do that, we've got to have leaders with the power to act fast and not to be hampered. And we have just such leaders and we are not hampering them. They are acting for us, we can see that every day, and we trust them, so we are acting with them.

We don't want to hamper them with some "political system"—whatever that may mean. What they are doing, all of it so far, is just what we want them to be doing. We're in the middle of all this construction of the new Cuba that we're already so proud of. So it's no trouble for us to forget all about this "political system." That's just an old abstraction to us—when it doesn't mean the government of thieves like with Batista. We've got plenty of liberty—we've got it for the first time—the real liberty. We are acting it out, not just talking about it.

Today all our moments of truth live as truth only to some, in the lower half of the Americas, the southern half, the exploited, the diseased, the impoverished half. To the northern half—to your half—these are not moments of truth at all. They are moments of peril. Maybe some of the perils are real. But some you imagine. The Yankees have no taste for the velocity and the violence of the revolution.

But the politics of The Other America, of our America, is increasingly going to be the politics of the guerrilla, the politics of the underground, and then the politics of economic and educational development. We are proving that these can be combined. We are proving that under tyranny of the sort that prevails in much of Latin America, and under the imperialism of the North

American sort that now prevails generally in Latin America, there is no other way.

V

The peril of our revolution is the peril of all revolutions.

The peril is that its moment of truth will become an epoch of lies.

Then the revolution would be over, and its glory turned into the empty, everyday misery.

Then we Cubans would have to fight again!

And we would win again, too!

But now we feel so strong, we feel so free, we feel so new, that we are not afraid to worry with you out loud.

Will Cuba be a different country in ten years? Of that there can be no doubt, if only because by then the children of illiterate peasants, now entering our new schools will be the leaders and the rank and file of Cuba. That is why at this moment all political organizations, strong as they may be, seem so provisional. This next generation will be the first generation to come to adulthood knowing anything but tyranny and poverty, disease and ignorance.

It is because we know this that some of us are beginning to worry about two things we've not yet had time to worry about much. These things are politics and culture. The reason they are important to us is because if we succeed in securing our sovereignty militarily, and if we succeed in establishing a real economic basis for our sovereignty, then these two things are going to determine what kinds of men and women, what kinds of human beings the Cubans of the quite immediate future are going to be. So let us consider with you these worries—first, in this letter, the political; in our next letter, the cultural.

Is our Cuba today a revolutionary dictatorship?

Yes, we suppose it is. But to understand what this means, in the case of Cuba at least, you must understand several things about this word and about Cuba. In the most literal sense imaginable, Cuba is a dictatorship of, by, and for the peasants and the workers of Cuba. That phrase, "dictatorship of workers and peasants," was turned into a lie by Stalin and under Stalinism. Some of us know that. But none of us is going about our revolution in that way. So, to understand us, you must try to disabuse yourself of certain images and ideas of "dictatorship." It is the pre-Stalin meaning of the phrase that is accurate for Cuba.

Its political meaning is this: that to carry through an economic revolution and to meet the external menace that you Yankees make for us, any political *system,* would seriously hamper us. Everything is fluid in Cuba now and everything is at stake. Very little is consolidated in the sense of having become the routine of some institution, and almost no political institutions have been consolidated. It is in this fluidity and while confronting this menace that our revolutionary Government is putting through the educational, the military, and the economic construction at such a whirlwind pace.

Politically, as we've said, there is no question at all but that our revolutionary Government has behind it a revolutionary consensus of the immense majority of our population. This has come about, and it continues, because of two specific facts about our Cuban revolution:

Economically, there have been, and there continue to be, definite increases in our standard of living—and more than that, in our standards of hope. Not in five years, not next year, but today and tomorrow we are improving the way we are living. The evident consensus, which amazes everyone who comes to Cuba, rests then, first of all, upon the evident improvements in how we are living. Revolution is construction.

Militarily, this close agreement of government with people rests upon the felt menace of the Yankees to Cuba. It rests upon the simple fact that we Cubans do feel: "My country or my death."

Revolution is construction.

My country or my death.

These are not mere slogans we've written on our walls. If you'll forgive us, they are not lies, like your "campaign rhetoric." They are just plain facts in Cuba; they are just plain facts about Cuba. And they *are* the "politics" of Cuba today. Our politics, if need be, are the politics of the gun, and if we can avoid that, our politics are the politics of the economic and the educational construction of our country.

The Council of Ministers is the nearest thing to a congress we have, and we are very well satisfied with it.

INRA is the nearest thing to the structure of a state we have, and we are certainly very well pleased with it.

And at the head of both, as well as everywhere else, whenever he is needed, is Fidel Castro, and we certainly are very, very well pleased with him.

Much of what you think bad about our revolution is due to the menace we feel of your counterrevolution. That's what we are thinking. And because of that, above all, we are thinking that the only "minority views" now are counterrevolutionary views. There are no other minorities; not yet, at least. The immense majority are with us, and inside the revolution there *are* a variety of constructive differences.

What do you want us to do, Yankee: make an institution out of your counterrevolution?

But how do we distinguish counterrevolutionary from constructive alternatives? That's not so difficult to do: After the final fighting ceases, and as it ceases, many criteria will come out of the revolution itself, as our economic criteria have. But our first task is to exist, then to ask *how* we may exist. We're practical men, not theoreticians. And what we've got is working too well for everybody for anyone to want to change it now. Maybe that's not good enough, but that is what we are thinking.

VI

But these politics, some of us know, *are* a phase. There is certainly no reason to suppose that such revolutionary politics will be permanent. In fact, we know that our revolutionary power, based upon the evident consensus, upon the very direct relation between government and people, cannot be expected to endure forever. We know that sometime in the future we'll have to make the relations between government and people more systematic, that we'll have to create a political system.

We have no reason to believe that this political system, which will come about after our present phase is over, will necessarily be dictatorial. Our aim is going to be to make our Government independent of the persons who are exercising the power. We know that in the building and in the maintenance of a free political society, we must establish nonrevolutionary means of changing that society. We know that we must set up some way whereby our leaders can be peacefully selected and peacefully changed. And we know, too, that there must be genuine control over both of these processes by the people of Cuba.

These are big and real problems. The leaders of our revolution. and above all, Fidel Castro himself, are aware of them. What they are thinking is this: Our political system, whatever it turns out to be—will it not have to come out of the continued back-and-forth play, the continued experience of the people and the Government, of each with the other? The revolution, in short, must create its own political forms, just as it already is creating its own economic and social forms—about which we are now so happy.

And aren't you expecting a little too much to ask us to set up our political *system* now? First things first, and the first things are military and economic and educational. The first thing is the military and the economic survival of Cuba as a sovereign state. The first thing is the economic base for sovereignty and the educated people capable of running their own state and their own economy.

Moreover, we revolutionaries have just not had the time to think about the political system that, sometime in the future, we've got to build. We know that sooner or later we've got to confront the problem. But if we worried all the time about that, we couldn't have made our insurrection as we did. And we couldn't now be going ahead so fast with education and with economic construction.

You must realize, of course, that very few people in Cuba are thinking at all about this question of a political system. The farmers and the workers and the less educated people are not even yet aware of it. It's only some of the intellectuals and revolutionary leaders who are now beginning to think about it at all.

The revolution *is* still very young. The enthusiasm of the farmers and the workers is still rising high, and this should continue for quite some time, if only because of the menace you make for us. Without that outside pressure, probably the enthusiasm would last a shorter time, but, as things are, several years of such enthusiasm and of such work is not a silly expectation.

The second thing you should realize is that any political *system* is always a restraint on the quickness needed by any real revolution. If we had an organized political system, we could not have done the things we have done in such a short time. Any system would lower the velocity of the revolution.

Third, you ought to realize that Fidel Castro certainly does not promote any "cult of the individual." On the contrary, he is very much aware of this problem, and he becomes quite angry—we have seen it—when there is so much adulation of him. He tries very hard to shift the enthusiasm from himself to the revolution. Although he knows very well the enormous importance of his own leadership, he tries to make the revolutionary construction the big and great thing, rather than Fidel Castro. He promotes not the cult of the individual but the facts of the revolution.

But is not this a peril, to depend so much upon one man—and for this one man to have such power? Of course it is: he might be assassinated or become ill. When men seize an opportunity, they make history; this man has. And he is. He is the most directly radical and democratic force in Cuba. He has always appealed, at every juncture, to public opinion, on the TV and also in person. Before any problem is solved, Fidel spends long hours on the TV. In the last 18 months the power in

Cuba has rested upon the people. He explains and he educates, and after he speaks almost every doubt has gone away. Never before has such a force of public opinion prevailed for so long and so intimately with power. So close, for example, that even a weak rumor sends Fidel to the TV to refute it or to affirm it, to explain what it is all about. So long as Fidel is there, we are going to be all right. His speeches actually create the revolutionary consciousness—and the work gets done. It is fantastic to see how, as it goes along, the revolutionary process transforms one layer after another of the population. And always, there is Fidel's antibureaucratic personality and way of going about things, of getting things done, without red tape and without delay and in a thoroughly practical and immediate way.

He has truly been, we believe, an extraordinarily courageous and intelligent man. In the incubation and in the insurrectionary phases of the revolution we doubt that we could have made it without him. Had he not been *here,* and done and said what he did do and say, the history of Cuba would have been different. Surely he is among the small number of men in the 20th century who have been event-making. Many times in those months and years and days just past, he *was* the revolution.

But we know he cannot *be* the revolution very much longer. There are too many things to be done. Events accumulate too rapidly. Now the front is too many-sided. Everything is in a new and different phase.

VII

Every revolutionary faces the fact that no revolution can last forever. Sooner or later he faces the fact of the next phase, after the black-or-white days. There comes a time when you're not just camping out any more, when the simple, heroic virtues are not enough, if only because the people, no matter how heroic, grow weary. The damned problems of consolidating, and of furthering, the revolutionary gains—these are different problems than those of camping out and making the insurrection.

And in our case, in the case of Cuba, these new problems are immensely more difficult than the camping out.

Because of the epoch in which our revolution occurs, we must not only master Cuban difficulties, but world difficulties and confusions.

Because of the peculiarities of the old Cuban economy, to overcome these difficulties, perhaps we are going to have to achieve some international position more workable than the one we are now assuming. We'll see.

But are you going to do anything to help us?

In the meantime, you just have to come up to the facts about what kind of a man Fidel Castro is, and what kinds of men the forty-or-so *commandantes* and the two-hundred-or-so *capitans* and the Council of Ministers—all those who make up the revolutionary Government of Cuba today—what kinds of men they really are. They have a real respect for the people and a real belief in the people. It's not some romantic idea. It's just something they know and something they are. These are the people—we revolutionaries think—and so you trust them. These are the people—and they can learn very fast what has to be done.

We suppose it's a little frightening to some of you, at least at first, when you've seen this revolutionary contact of revolutionary people with revolutionary leaders. You've never seen that in North America, at least not for a long time.

Probably, part of why it works so well is that after all Cuba is a small and compact country. Maybe it wouldn't work at all, maybe it would turn into something else, something very bad, if it came about in a big, organized country like yours. We don't know. All we know is that here it is working.

Everybody now in command, as we've said, is a custodian until the young cadres grow up and take over. But—you may say—these people in command are training the cadres. That's true, but the cadres are also training themselves, if only because things are not too well or too tightly organized. In part, too, all of us, young and younger, are being trained by the very thrust and drive of the revolutionary process, and all the new institutions that are being created by the revolution every week.

So, are our *commandantes* military dictators? Totalitarian commanders? Whatever your answer may be, for us these words are just meaningless abstractions. Economic and military powers are in their hands; complete political power as well, including what you call judicial appeal. If there are difficulties about land problems, any differences of opinion about such things, the matter comes into their offices and they solve it right then and there. Don't you see they have to: we've got to plant that land.

But the abstract idea of a totalitarian dictatorship is certainly far removed from the realities of what these men actually are doing and how the people behave with them. They work and drive and fly about their INRA zones without any guards, and everywhere, with the greatest familiarity they are greeted with genuine affection that could not be pretended. In the most idealistic meaning of the term, this is "a dictatorship of the people." Nobody feels any need for your "mechanisms of popular control," because what these men are doing is so obviously, so immediately, so fully in line with the felt interests and needs of the people at large. The results of their actions are so immediately good, who can argue that they as men are not good?

Above all, we believe neither Fidel Castro nor any other of our revolutionary leaders will use force to maintain himself in power. Certainly he does not have to now. That is one reason we revolutionaries are so preoccupied with things that have to do with the immediate welfare of the people. We are not sacrificing one generation now for future generations. Think of all the public beaches. Think of all the motels and all the other immediately good things that we are building. Think of the modern hatcheries and chicken farms: those are not "one-shot" gifts. They are productive facilities. Who can argue it's not good that people living on the strips of land between the back road and the cane field, without any land themselves, without any work or health, without any hope for the future, but a future of deadening misery—these people are moving into the new rural homes with tile floors and showers and toilets in them, and filtered water? It is they who are producing those chickens. And that is every bit as much a part of our "totalitarianism" as is the abstract political notion of dictatorship.

Remember, we are not going through any Stalinist kind of forced industrialization. Remember, too, how flexible our consumption on this semitropical island can be: we can live on less, if we have to. Remember, finally, that we are more fortunate than the Russians were, and even the Chinese, because *they* will certainly help us economically.

Our very lack of any political system has been working in a most direct and democratic way. We don't know what you mean by the word "democratic," but if what we're doing isn't democratic, then we don't want democracy. And if you *identify* "the free society" with what you've got in North America, please know that we don't. We've tried that kind of a political system in Cuba. Maybe it works for you—that's your business; it certainly did not work for us.

Also, we are not so dogmatic as many of you seem to be. We are not among those who assert that *only* under the particular system such as you have can men be free. We can quite well imagine real freedom, for example, in the Soviet Union in the future. But that really isn't the point.

You ought to realize by now that our old politics is one big reason we don't think about "politics" much today, and don't want to: when we think of politics we think of the corruption in the old congress and how many senators and representatives there were, and how they all got rich out of it while we rotted away. *That* was a politics for robbers and tyrants and rich men. But not for us. All that politics wore the mask of "democracy," please remember. All the trappings were there, the constitution, the parties, the elections—but all of it was just a big front without any liberty and with no food to eat. Because of this fact, very naturally, we think that all of that kind of system may well be mere nonsense, and this idea is underlined by our judgment of the United States system of democracy, which— please remember—is solely in terms of what it has meant for us Cubans.

VIII

The problem of our political system is, of course, the problem of freedom, of its meanings and its conditions. We do not know the answers to these problems. Like many other people, and even some politicians, we revolutionaries are working on them all the time. But the truth, we think, is that thinkers who have never been political actors, are not going to solve them. And the political actors of the overorganized nations such as the United States, and perhaps the Soviet Union, are not going to solve them, either.

The problem of freedom is an ultimate question. The first thing to be said about it is that *nobody* in the world has really solved it and that nobody is going to solve it once and for all. By its very nature, it is something that goes on. Its solution *is* its continuing to go on.

In our situation, given what we've come out of, and given what we now face, we've got to get started before we can continue—and that has, and probably will continue for a while to require: revolution. Revolution is a wrenching loose from the old order. It is the destruction of the main institutions, and much of the psychology of the old order, and then a lot of daring new beginnings. And all this, of course, is our perilous road.

All over the world political actors and people who have newly come out of political un-freedom of the plainest and most awful sort, out of social sloth and economic slavery and biological misery—all over the world, they are the ones who are searching out various new roads to various new kinds of freedom. They are perilous roads, but they are also possible roads to freedom; that is one reason they are so perilous.

And that is something you in the United States—as a government and as a people—are *not* doing. Neither your leaders nor your people feel the need of it. They assume they're already there, that they've already got it—this freedom. Rather than that, perhaps, they've already had it.

But we don't want to argue about all that here. We bring it up only to suggest that it is because of their provincial, dead-end smugness that Yankee politicians and officials and many of your intellectuals, too, have such difficulties understanding what people like us are really all about and what we are up against. What we are all about, we think, is the search for new roads to new kinds of freedom—and what we are up against are obstacles of which The Founding Fathers of the Yankee Republic never dreamed, much less had nightmares about.

By what we do, we are either going to solve these new problems of new freedoms under new conditions, or we are going to smash the chance even to raise the old problems. And there is the peril of it: that we'll not have the imagination or the guts—and it's going to take plenty of both—to avoid just falling back on all the old ways of dodging the issues, deferring them, double-talking them away, or setting up a glittering big façade for more subtle tyrannies than men have ever known.

We know that if we have avoided the stupid old Latin American kind of military dictatorship, we have not therefore avoided the perils of dictatorship.

We know that although we are throwing off alien economic domination we have not therefore avoided the perils of imperialism.

There are many forms of dictatorship There are many kinds of imperialism.

But there are many kinds of freedom, too, and a variety of roads to each of them, not just one obvious road. We've got to find, we've got to invent, as we go along, Cuba's road to Cuba's freedom.

But from whom or from what can we learn? First of all, of course, from Cuba's own new experiences. But doesn't history provide any lessons for us, for the 26th of July Movement, for Cuba? To the extent that we really succeed, to that extent, no, history doesn't help much. For what we'll be doing will be new.

But of course there are guideposts set up by history, signs of roads to various dead-ends, signs to roads that are impassable by the Cuban vehicle, signs of roads washed out and never rebuilt. Most of the so-called lessons of history are object lessons. They come as injunctions reading "don't." But even those, as we know, are often silly.

Still, revolutionaries do have to try to use whatever history may mean for them. We think we've already drawn one sound conclusion from it: we cannot learn much from the Yankee establishment.

For the Cuban past, the U.S. system has meant: economic domination by corporations and Cuban poverty and all the rest of it.

For the Cuban present, we think it means: a counter-revolutionary force to our Cuban revolution.

For the Cuban future, we think it means: no promise whatsoever. The U.S. system is not exportable to Cuba; the results of it inside the U.S.A., however they may be judged, are not exportable to inside Cuba.

We don't know that a congress, a two-party state, elections every four years—we don't know that these are the only and the indispensable ways to freedom. Nor do you. Nor does anybody else. But to believe that only these *are* freedom is indeed to be an idiot of abstractions, an historical provincial, and an unwarranted pessimist.

IX

But, you may ask: Are we aware enough of the experience of previous revolutions? Do we really know about the perilous road of any revolution in any hungry nation?

We hope there will be more and more people in the revolutionary Government who are preoccupied with this. You must realize—think now of our situation—that since the early fifties we've been making the revolution, and we have not been able to read and to study, as we should have done. Most of us did most of our reading before 1952 or 1953, and nothing much since then. We're only about thirty now, you must remember. But these days we are trying to catch up. After our work, many of us devote two or three hours to study. We also want very much to travel, in many other countries. This is one of our main preoccupations.

Our lack of knowledge we must now make up for by reasoning. What else have we got? But maybe it's good that we've been ignorant. If Fidel had been an army general, he'd not have been able to do what he did. His very lack of experience was of great value. Sometimes knowledge or experience itself is a wall that stops people, instead of a starting point. With us, being what we are, it's a starting point.

In the meantime, we think we should delay the establishment of any fixed political system. The question is, where is the stopping point of such a policy? And one answer is:

When the Cuban people are not preoccupied with these big issues of military safety and economic security, then we revolutionaries will know, as we have known before, what the people want. When that time comes, it will be in the air. You can feel it. It is heavy on your shoulders. This is a government very close to the people. Remember that, please. It is a solid fact of the Cuban revolution.

But what system will it be? No one can answer that. But we believe that whatever our political system will turn out to be, it will not look like any known political system.

That is true, first of all, because of Fidel's personality: he does not know limits, he has a genuine originality. Ours will be a simple, practical, flexible system, we are sure of that. And it will take fully into itself the opinions of the people. Of course, we believe that minorities should have the means of expressing their opinions. For what is a political system but a way of protecting minority opinions? Otherwise, it is a dictatorship. We Cuban revolutionaries certainly know that! We must get the opinions of the people probably not just by their numbers but by the fields of activities they are in. The people must be represented in terms of their needs. And in our system we must develop a better coordination of the three traditional powers of government.

One thing that will influence our political system a great deal is our economic planning and our Government's control of our economics. Any underdeveloped economy that is really on the move shows you right away the need for such control: to avoid the waste of resources, if for no other reason. And for speed. There is so much to do and so little to do it with, really. The greatest crime today in Cuba is to waste our resources. So the economy *must* be planned by our Government. And this will, of course, be a main determining factor of our political system, whatever it turns out to be.

So, by the time the question of our political system really arises among us, we hope to have in hand solutions to it, and to make something fine politically here in Cuba, as we are already doing economically.

We Cuban revolutionaries know that like all men who have done the sort of thing we have done, we are no longer "just men." We are also a kind of symbol. To this symbol we ourselves must respond; to it, we also are now beholden. We cannot altogether control the symbol that we have become. It is in the hands of too many of us. But every act, every sentence, every decision we make does and will affect that symbol. And that symbol—The Cuban Revolution—is important, not only for Cuba, but to all the peoples of the hungry-nation bloc. Now we must act in full awareness of all these facts, in full awareness of all these peoples, and with continuing passionate concern for all the perils before the peoples of the hungry-nation bloc.

For what we have already done, no matter what happens next, we believe that "history" will indeed "absolve" us. But neither history nor our own biographies are yet done, and their interplay, that too is as yet in perilous balance. We're becoming aware of that as our revolution moves on. Neither you, nor we, nor any other men can yet know whether we are going to be up to the terrible and glorious responsibilities that are ours.

The revolution is not a permanent form of society— we know that. But these problems of politics are not our immediate problems. Many other problems are immediate; they are urgent. And they are taking up all our time. We don't know how long we're going to be under such a fierce pressure of events. But it is absolutely obvious to us that we are going to solve these political problems just as we are solving the economic and social and military problems of Cuba—in a Cuban way. We fight now to exist. We feel we're in a life-or-death struggle—with your Government—and you haven't permitted us to face these institutional worries that you bring up.

So here's one final thing you surely must realize by now: These "pressures of events" we spoke of, which keep us from even thinking much now about our future political system—your North American Government and your Yankee monopolies are in very large part responsible for them. And if you keep it up, if you increase the pressure, well then, we won't have as good a chance to work out a political system of the kind we'd very much like to. If you keep us on military edge, we'll have to be military too; if you keep trying to hurt us economically, we'll have to put more of our energies into just economic existence. So, in either case, we'll have less energy and less chance to work out a political system. Please do think about this, Yankee. Perhaps then, if you've any political sense, you'll know what you ought to do.

SEVEN

CULTURE IN CUBA

We are a generation of revolutionary actors, but as we've been working in our revolution, we have come to see the necessity for intellectual preparation. We know well the need for real intellectual work, and we are developing the capacities for it. We've realized the immediate need for the serious work of planning and organizing. But more than that: because of our restlessness, because of our inquietude, we've come upon the need for the all-round development of all our intellectual and moral capacities.

Our revolution *is* extraordinarily curious. In the old Cuba, we fought intellectual mediocrity, but in the first period, in the insurrection, we ourselves had a lack of real intellectual power. People saw in us then only the heroism, the bearded men with the high sentiments. They did not see our deep intellectual vocation. But it is very important to understand, as the revolution advances, how our worry for intellectual creation—which is so typical of all our modern world—also advances. And how, in Cuba, it is deepening.

The intellectual searches for truth; all that is artificial the real intellectual is against. The revolution, too, smashes whatever is mere artifice. So it is only, we think, in a revolutionary epoch that intellectuals can do their real work, and it is only by intellectual effort that revolutionaries can be truly successful. In these terms, of all the big revolutions, the most real, we think, is ours. The revolution in Cuba has been initiated, if ever one was, by young intellectuals. It is in considerable part due to worries of an intellectual's kind.

Knowing now how many Cubans are still illiterate, knowing that we are only now setting up primary-grade schools, you may think we really are crazy when we tell you that we aim to establish in Cuba the finest intelligentsia in the Western Hemisphere or in the world. But we are very serious when we say that. In our educational system, we are going to gather up all the young children from the impoverished and illiterate corners of Cuba—all that hitherto wasted talent—and with them we're going to establish in Cuba an intellectual and ·a cultural life of a sort most people in the world have ceased even to dream of.

We think that much sooner than you could expect, the problem of culture will be central in Cuba—and in the world attention given to Cuba. At the moment, "culture" is very much education, necessarily of a rudimentary sort; "culture" is now mainly the construction of a primary-school system, and the quick training of technicians and lower administrative personnel. But even so, "What are all these people going to be taught?" we are asking ourselves as we build the schools. "What is going to be the cultural life of these hundreds of thousands of children who very soon won't be children?"

But let us tell you first about what we're doing, then about some of our problems, and then about some of our plans.

I

Alongside our military defense and our economic construction, there is our educational work, our third great task for this year! We aim, of course, to put good schools in every corner of Cuba. But we obviously can't do that all at once, if only because we have so many other problems which we must solve first. But what we're doing is to solve some of *those* "other problems" by means of our educational revolution.

Take, for example, the problem of unemployed youth —boys and girls between fourteen and eighteen years old who are living in our cities, who are uneducated, and who are idle. In May 1960 we began to set up what we call "brigades." First, a boy who wants to join is checked medically, and then he goes to the Sierra. There he climbs mountains, but he begins at once to study and to work. About 2,000 boys are now in school there, and by September 1960, 10,000 more will be in the Sierra; in 18 months, there will be some 80,000 such young people in the brigades.

You must realize that these boys have never had any chance to study, that they are too old to go to primary school with the children, and that they have no jobs. So we are training them—some for the handling of agricultural machinery, some to dust crops by airplanes and other means; we also have a special school for technicians and one for those who want to study forestry, because we have a very large forestry program already well under way.

We're setting up brigades for girls, too. The first school for them is already in operation. Many thousands of young women will be needed because, you see, we're going to put nurseries all over Cuba; then the sons and daughters of the workers and the farmers will be taken care of in these nurseries. These girls in the brigades, studying in the afternoon, will organize and run the nurseries. They will also make dresses for all the children and they will make clothes for all the brigades, for the boys and for themselves. It used to be that the only places the poor girls from the country could go was into the bars, and from there, many would drift into prostitution. Or they would go into the houses of the rich as servants. But now they are going into schools, into the girls' brigades. All this is something of a stopgap, of course, to salvage this generation, because in the future, you realize, there will be regular schools all over Cuba for all the children of Cuba.

But in the meantime, the brigade solves several problems of this lost youth at once: It gives them a chance at some kind of education they thought they'd never have; it helps solve the general problem of unemployment in a useful way because they will work in the mornings and go to school in the afternoons; it avoids the old "solution" of delinquency for such youth; and, of course, it helps build up the economy and the educational institutions of Cuba.

We have also set up a voluntary teacher system. In the old order our old teachers were from the city, and they wouldn't go out into the rural districts. Now, of course, girls from among the rural poor are being brought into our new system of teacher training, but what we've done, as an immediate measure, is quite radical. Cuba has about 5,000 people with a higher education who have volunteered to go to the Sierra as teachers. They are in training for three months there. Then they will begin to teach. These voluntary teachers have been taught a new system for the teaching of reading and writing. In September 1960 they will go to the far-off places in the backward mountains. In the course of their work there, they will pick out the most talented boys and girls, and these children will go to school in the cities. We are gathering our future intelligentsia, you see, from the far places in Cuba. We do not want to waste *any* of our talent.

The voluntary teachers are now preparing themselves in the Sierra. After their training, some will teach in the brigades; others will teach our rebel soldiers; some will work with the rural militia; and some will be in the regular schools that we are setting up.

But the one thing we are perhaps the proudest of is our school cities in the Sierra. There will be ten such cities in all, when we are through with the building, and some 20,000 students in each. The first unit is already in operation. But why a school *city?* Because in those rural, mountainous areas, the people are so scattered that it's not really possible to build regular schools in such a way that they are convenient. Just as many things cannot be done economically and reasonably unless you have a larger unit, in like manner you cannot educate these children of the Sierra unless you bring them together and build a larger unit for them. That is why we have the school cities. Also, as we've said, teachers don't like to go into the backwoods, and that is being solved by the school city, which will of course have a complete round of civilized life. Fidel selected the site for the first school city while he was still fighting in the mountains, and now it is there.

The children work in the mornings, and in the afternoons they study. We believe that children like to work at light tasks. They like to know where their rice comes from. When we were boys nobody told us why we had rice, or where it came from. There will be teachers of the small boys, and professors who will teach the teachers, and we are arranging it so the older children will teach the younger children. The little students will have cows, sheep, and pigs, and some will go to the fishery to become fishery experts. Of course, the children will take care of their own food, cleaning, and so on. Also, small industries are being established and the students will in this way pay their own way. There will be a school for nurses, for example, and those students of nursing will work in the hospital that we will need there.

Our teachers believe that they can choose the most talented children at about the time they are ten years old. So that is the time that the most talented will be selected for more specialized training and given scholarships to the university.

You know already, don't you, that every one of the six largest military garrisons from the old Batista order, as well as the most notoriously evil police station in Havana, have now been made over into schools? The old Pentagon of Cuba now houses the Ministry of Education. And we're building rural schools, of course, in every corner of Cuba we can reach. We're not finished, we're only beginning our educational construction.

II

Where can we learn useful things? For example, very soon we are going to be setting up a medical plan, a health program for all the Cuban people. Can we learn anything from you Yankees about that? We think: absolutely nothing. We think *your* medical system—your businessman doctors and drug companies and ridiculously expensive hospitals and medical schools for the rich— we think all that is a set of rackets and excuses for not having any real and humane and sensible health program.

But can we learn from the Russians about the organization of a health program? It is certainly possible. We'd like to know more about it.

But the fact is we already know what we need to do. In a word, all we've got to do is the opposite of the old medical rackets in Cuba.

In the old order, it took seven years after high school to become an M.D., but all these people were called "surgeons," even if they had never seen an operation. Sometimes they would go to a town and start operating at once, often never having done it before. It wasn't so unusual to have four out of five appendicitis cases die. There were abortion rings involving Havana physicians, linked to the United States, of course. That's why we have to be hard. No more abortions. We will simply expel the butchers from practice altogether. When our good doctors had to operate on a woman with a perforated uterus from a mangled abortion, they reported this to the judge, but the judge would tell them to be quiet, that some big shots were protecting this practice. If, nevertheless, they appealed to the Havana court, up higher, nothing came of it. They had rackets here with everything. The drug companies gave new automobiles to a doctor who prescribed only their drugs, and some doctors owned the local pharmacy, so it was all one racket together. That's why we have to be hard.

In the old order, the medical career was very much coveted as a quick way to get rich. A doctor can do favors for people, treating their illnesses cheaply, and hence a political career was open to him. A great many senators and the mayors of towns were doctors. The legal career was also a similar setup.

But we do not think it is so difficult to establish a civilized health program. First, you must realize that the phrase "socialized medicine" is a ghost. Second, you must realize that doctors are not little tin gods, but highly specialized repair men: it only takes four or five years after high school to train such a man quite well; maybe more for medical research, but that will come. Third, you must set up a plan whereby medical services and personnel are brought to where the people are in need of them—not just in Havana.

Our principle will be that if you make a thousand dollars a month, then you should pay maybe $200 for an operation, but that if you make a hundred dollars a month, you should pay nothing. And a doctor, of course, ought to be on some kind of reasonable salary, so he can be a doctor, and not a profit-maker off people who are sick.

You think it is not that simple? Wait a bit, and you will see it in Cuba. A lot of things are simple in a civilized society, once you get rid of the silly abstractions that hide the economic truths of life. It won't take us more than four or five months to get our medical program going well. The plans we've already made. So probably you'll be reading soon all about The Red Medicine System in Cuba. When you do, remember about all the old medical rackets (some of them, we are told, you still have—why don't you get rid of them, Yankee?). And remember, too, about the illness and disease of the old Cuba that nobody did anything about.

III

Now, you must realize that the old Cuba really had no culture or science and very few establishments in which a Cuban culture might develop. Culturally and intellectually, as well as educationally, we were a mixed-up colony. As for our institutions: take just two of them briefly: the press and the university in Havana.

In the late fifties there were about 100 radio stations, more than 20 newspapers, and some six TV channels. At that time, the press was just a part of Batista's ruling gang. All these media of communication led a highly artificial life, for of course there were not enough resources in Cuba to maintain all these newspapers and radio stations. But they were not ordinary information and entertainment media, they were built around persons who had other businesses and who used them to protect their interests, and then too Batista subsidized them in various ways. Let us tell you about one case.

There was a man who was a friend of Mussolini. When Italian fascism was defeated he came to the Americas. In the Santo Domingo Republic he was in business with Trujillo. He left there, came to Cuba, and set up a business here. Sometimes he ran into difficulties in Cuba, so he also established businesses in Argentina and elsewhere. He had a connection with a general somewhere, and also with the Italian Mafia. Then he bought a big news-paper, *El Mundo,* and also radio and TV channels. He established some 43 businesses here in Cuba—from sell-ing Cadillacs to rich Cubans to the smuggling of drugs. He was in on the black market for dollars. Now, of course, his whole illegal world has been discovered and exposed by the revolution. The files of all these busi-nesses are now somewhere in the Office for the Recupera-tion of Stolen Property. But that is the kind of man who was running one of our biggest newspapers.

As for Havana U., it was a prehistoric institution, full of all the old vices of the old Cuba. Of course, there were exceptions, but they were mainly the students' doing —despite the university, not because of it. Like many other universities in Latin America, it didn't really have much to do with the real educational needs of the coun-try. Havana U. didn't train the technicians and engineers that Cuba really needed, but of course they couldn't: there wouldn't have been any jobs for graduates to work at even if they had been trained. Many of "the professors" weren't professors at all. They were friends and relatives of the powerful who were given "legates." Many didn't teach, but passed out mimeographed lecture notes or "copies," as we called them. There was a lot of dull memorizing, but there wasn't much real learning. Cer-tainly, it wasn't exactly a brilliant center of Cuban in-tellectual and cultural life.

Yankee journalists have written much about how the students have brought the revolution to Havana U. They haven't written about *what* was being revolutionized: a prehistoric institution. We'll have to do better than that for our new Cuba. And we're going to. We're starting out with all the disorder that we've inherited, and with what amounts to No Culture In Cuba. To bring about real cultural and intellectual establishments is one of our biggest and most difficult tasks. Of course, it's linked, as we've said, with our need for administrators and techni-cians in the new Cuba. But we want much more than that. We want poetry as well as physics. And we know you can't plan for poets as you can for engineers. You can only plan and construct cultural institutions, and

then hope that poets, as well as engineers, will grow in
them and do great work.

Now, as we've already told you, because our revolution has been made without a long revolutionary process, we've lacked skilled and tested personnel. If you
add to that the fact of such inadequate educational and
cultural institutions in prerevolutionary Cuba, you begin
to see our problem.

But also, please consider that all this has contrib-
uted to the revolution. Sometimes the naïve can see the
truth better than the oversophisticated. Still, our great
need is to train future generations to meet problems.
Only a tiny minority went to the old university, and
when they got there nobody taught them to see any of
the realities of Cuba or of the world. So, now, that's
another reason we have this problem of personnel, why
it is so important. But we will solve it! Cuban reality
and Cuban difficulties rest in part on the total failure of
education in the old Cuba. Take the procedure for select-
ing high-school teachers, for example. Before the revolution, there were no examinations, and it was a matter
of graft or hit-or-miss who got to be a teacher. The
strictly educational qualifications have had to be lowered
by the revolutionary Government, as well as the qualifications for the inspector of the grade schools. There are
simply not enough university teachers now for the university. Perhaps there are a dozen real university professors in Cuba. We are trying to get such people
from other Latin American countries, and technical people, too, from such places as Poland. Again, you must
realize that lack of personnel is characteristic of all countries with political and economic conditions like Cuba's.
That's why some people think, with justification, too,
that we're making such a primitive revolution, and that's
why the impulses of popular emotion push all other
things before them.

IV

We know that for any culturally impoverished country
like Cuba this problem of establishing cultural institu-

tions is a terribly important and a perilous effort. We'd like to say too that we don't think anybody in the world has really solved the problem of establishing the best chances for art and literature and culture in general.

On the one hand, there's your capitalist way of doing it. It's a commercial establishment of culture. If it will sell, then it will be produced—pictures, or soap, or a course in changing the baby's diaper, or poems, or soap opera. For the rest, perhaps some rich foundation may support it, and if so, good. But there is no real plan, no real establishment of cultural effort—except the commercial.

We don't think we can afford to go about it in that way. We are too much in need of it, and we can't afford to be so wasteful of the talent and resources we do have.

On the other hand, there's the Soviet way—state or party control of all cultural activity, directly or indirectly. Perhaps that's all right in science and technology—as for that, it's not so very different from your science and technology establishments—but we don't think it has resulted in much good poetry. They sometimes seem to be getting better, but still not good enough for us. We aim to do better. We want our new cultural establishments to be part of our revolution, and so, like the revolution itself, we want them to be free and useful and beautiful and fluent.

So we are thinking about it now, debating quietly among ourselves this great social problem of culture, of art, of literature, of the cinema, and how to really do something fine with TV.

As in all our thinking, we start with the felt need to consolidate our revolution, to protect it from whatever menaces it. The only real and true consolidation, of course, is the creation by the revolution itself of new kinds of men and women. And that is where the problem of culture comes into it. The revolution must create a social order that is not menaced by the old reactionary views. And those old views, we think, *have* often been served by art and culture. Race prejudice, for example. Whatever one thinks about free art, it seems to us that no art can be both free and effective in a society that isn't free, and that means to us a society without privilege. So in a revolution, we say to ourselves, must not art enroll itself in this struggle to win and to consolidate a free society? Along with that, we remember that the people cannot yet decide well what is of excellence and what is not. And so, as revolutionaries, we worry that art could, that it might, hurt the revolution. So maybe we just have to limit artistic expression.

Remember now, please, this is only one line of our thought; we'll tell you the other in a moment. We are just thinking frankly and out loud with you.

You must remember that first and above all we are revolutionaries, that we have fought hard, and that now we have won many hard battles. You must realize, too, that even as we acted in this revolutionary drama, with our hands filled with big jobs and our minds filled with great objectives, we were thinking too of the heroes among us, of our brothers, who fell. All that human tragedy and glory of the revolution, and the essential humanity of our struggle, and then the struggle once accomplished, its human fruits—why should not all that become the objects of art and literature? Why should not art, through its many different forms of expression, gather all that up for the present and for the future generations? For is not art an instrument whereby the consciousness of men is formed? Does not art in that way serve humanity? And we revolutionaries do want humanity to know what we have done and what we are doing.

Must not art pay a tribute to the revolution?

But then, we ask ourselves too, must not the revolution, especially our Cuban revolution, pay a tribute to art? And what is that tribute? What must it be?

Are you beginning to see our problem with culture in Cuba?

We want an absolutely free manifestation of the human spirit. That is our goal. We want a great and absolutely free intelligentsia. Up in the Sierra, nobody told us in which style we must act. Just so, men must write and paint freely. That liberty we revolutionaries have breathed; it is not some abstraction to us. It is what we have breathed in the streets, in the mountains, it is everywhere here in Cuba, everywhere that there is revolution.

But then, we think to ourselves, what are the conditions in a revolutionary period that permit this absolutely free culture to flourish? Do such conditions, can such conditions exist in a revolution? First, there is the internal fight of interests—the revolution and the counterrevolution. Then there is the external menace—the counterrevolution with which your Government threatens us. These create a great tension of mind and spirit, and in that revolutionary tension it is difficult to see the conditions for an absolutely free culture. It is a great dilemma for us.

Perhaps this is the only answer possible: The less the revolution feels menaced, the more chemically pure will be the liberty of expression in Cuba. When we no longer feel that we must fight to exist, then—to that extent —we will be able to think well about the freedom of culture and expression. We have faith that the Cuban revolution embodies full liberty, a liberty that men have never before known. The less we have to struggle merely to exist, the more we can ask freely *how* we want to exist, and the more the climate will prevail in which a full and free variety of answers to that ultimate question can be given, and debated, and thought about by all the people of Cuba.

If that is not so good an answer to the problem of culture, it is the truth about our circumstances, our worries, and our hopes.

V

But let us tell you about one hope some of us have— not all of us, but some—these days. We want, as we've already said, to make revolutionary Cuba into a real intellectual and cultural center of the world. We know well that all new cultural beginnings today must be part of world culture; that no truly intellectual life can occur if the mind is restricted; that no art can have genuine and lasting value if it is not in a universal language. East and West, God knows there is enough restriction, enough laziness of stereotypes. Smash them, we say to ourselves. And the only way to do that is to open up a true world forum that is absolutely free. As our revolution is consolidated, that forum will become the vanguard of our society. It will be the seed bed of the future. It will be the climate in which new minds can form themselves, and then solve problems we don't yet even know about.

So why not go about this directly, as we have gone about our economic and educational construction, and everything else so far? What we are thinking of is the establishment in Havana of a university with a worldwide faculty. We want to hear in these new halls of learning a Chinese Communist Party member discussing with a North American Republican Party member the meanings of freedom! Let a Polish economist discuss with a Cuban economist the problems of the collectivization of land. Let a Mexican oil expert discuss the issues of nationalization of oil resources with a Venezuelan expert, employed by Standard Oil of New Jersey. Let a British Labor Party man discuss with a Yugoslav politician—whatever they want to discuss.

And put it all on tape. Print it in the newspapers of Cuba. Make it available in translations for the press of the world. Make books out of it. Make Cuban intellectual life a truly international, a truly free forum, for the *entire* range of world opinion, study, art, judgment, feeling.

The Yankees are afraid of "Communists," and so their universities are not really free.

The Russians are afraid of "anti-Communists," and so their universities are not really free.

We Cubans aren't afraid of any idea: so we are going to be really free. We want a university in which there is no hysterical nonsense about communism *or* about anticommunism. And is it not one of the urgent, the next steps of the Cuban revolution? It is urgent for inside Cuba—because we do need expert help in our educational and cultural efforts; and it is urgent for Cuba's relations with each and every part of the world—because we are not as yet well understood.

If we could do this, who could then say that the Cuban revolution was not indeed establishing a new zone of a new freedom in the Americas?

If this cultural and intellectual center should come

about, how then could men of small minds and narrow
views—formed in the old Cuba, after all—how could
they come to prevail with all their rigid silliness and
dogmatism and provinciality?

If such a university should come about in Havana,
who then could say that Cuba's moment of truth was
going to end up as an epoch of lies?

But to get down to it: how could we get the faculty
members to come to Havana for—say—a two-year period? Of course, we would pay them a regular salary for
their work; but we know that good people everywhere
are busy, and that it's a great deal of trouble to pack up
and go anywhere for a year or two. So we would offer
them special inducements.

In a word, we'd set up with and for that faculty a
little international city!

That's the way we Cuban revolutionaries go about
things. Perhaps we could house them all in one of the
big hotels—perhaps the Riviera would do. There we'd
have a polylingual kindergarten and primary-grade school
for all their children, as well as for the children of the
Cubans on the faculty. In the classrooms and elsewhere
we'd set up those U.N.-type simultaneous translation outfits, and we would provide for each man or woman who
did not know Spanish a tutor for a couple of hours a
day at first, and of course we'd have small language
classes in several languages for those who wanted to attend them. There is no end to the kinds of opportunities
for everyone involved that we Cubans could make out of
all the problems that our idea involves.

But there's one problem those of us who are thinking
about this idea must face: would the Yankee professors
and intellectuals and artists, would the Yankees come?
Would top-flight Yankee economists "recognize" Red
China's top-flight economists, and so discuss with them
the economic problems of the world?

Would some of the best U.S. intellectuals—whoever
they are, if they are—would they come to Dangerous
Red Cuba?

Of course, we could do it without the Yankees, but
it would be ever so much better with them. We do want

it to be truly international. We think the Russians and the Chinese and many other people would be glad to take part in it, but would you Yankees?

As a matter of fact, this would cost something—although not as much as you might think. There is much wealth in the U.S.A.—in foundations, for example. Why don't they *help* us to do this great thing? Don't they see that we do have a problem of culture, and that it is now, and that they could help us solve it?

VI

Then why in the name of all that's true, good, and beautiful, don't some of you help us to solve this terribly important problem of the culture of Cuba?

Now our revolution is just entering the phase in which high intellectual qualities come to be needed most. Perhaps this is our peril, but it is also our chance. We do need help of a practical kind from intellectuals everywhere. All that we ask is that they be honest observers and straight thinkers, and that they try their best to understand us and our revolution—in its own terms, at first, and then in any terms they choose.

There are many young men among us now having great responsibilities. What they do or fail to do may, in all truth, determine the future of Cuba. They know this, and they know too that often they are not well prepared. But they are very eager to learn, they are open for good preparation. Soon they will be able to prepare themselves as Cuban education and cultural institutions become established.

But it is in the establishment of all this that we could use help. That help *could* make the difference between an epoch of truth or an epoch of lies.

But your U.S. intellectuals do nothing. Again, they are out of it. They hesitate. Don't they see that they can act on their own, that they don't have to wait for U.S. Government grants or Ford Foundation fellowships? Don't they know that as intellectuals they are free men who can come to Cuba` and do great work? Don't they know that in doing this they would learn far more than they could possibly teach?

Or don't they want to compete intellectually in the world today? When some of our rural Cuban youths came back from the Latin American Youth Congress in Havana, they were amazed at how much many of those youths from other countries knew. But your youth was not even there. Maybe your college students don't have anything to tell us, or to the other peoples of the world, that is worth listening to—and maybe they know it! Well, we are going to learn from whomever we can; if not you —then others.

It's a big world, Yankee. Why don't you come out into it a bit? With your mind, we mean, not just with the money and the bombs and the self-blinding cry of the anti-Communist who wouldn't know a Yugoslav from a Chinese. Well, do your students know the difference of these two systems? Could they write a dozen decent pages about it? Could you—whoever you are?

But those *are* among the problems that interest us, and those are the problems that interest most of the world's youth today—which is, of course, the youth of the hungry nations. But you're in the world, too. Aren't you interested in it? We're interested in all the movements of Africa, and all the new nations that are coming up there. We're interested in the why of the extremes of utter poverty and fabulous wealth in the world. We're interested in the ideological debate between China and Russia today. We want to know just exactly what Nasser is doing in Egypt, and what's going to happen next in South Africa.

Aren't Yankee students and intellectuals interested in such things too? And where *are* all your tens of thousands of college students? Don't they want to mix into the world and find out about it personally? They certainly don't seem to, to us. At least at our school city in the Sierra—which, after all, *is* an exciting project for anyone who is young and alive—we don't notice the North American students.

Up there this summer there were 250 students from 45 countries, mostly from Latin America, but also from Europe—East and West, of course—who had come to work there. They paid their own way, many of them selling personal things to get the money for the trip. The

Cuban Government paid only their maintenance while they were in Cuba. We had architectural students from Bogotá, Colombia and ten such students from France and three or four from Italy. They all worked hard, digging foundations and constructing the schools. And our lady captain—Isabel Rielo is her name, and she is the head of the school city—she welcomed them all, you can be sure of that. "We are so happy," she said to these students from all over the world, "we feel this is the climax of all our years of effort."

But where were your tens of thousands of students? Where were they, with all the money they have? Don't they *feel* the excitement of all the worlds that are being created right under their eyes? Or were they just born tired out and bored and with no place to go and nothing to do?

Maybe they've read too much of what some of your intellectuals have written about the Cuban revolution. We don't mean now the stuff run about Cuba in the newspapers. That was expected. It is very important politically, but it has no intellectual or moral significance.

What we are talking about now are the highly intelligent, sophisticated reflections and reportage of liberals, and especially of those ex-radicals who at least verbally cling to socialist kinds of ideals, but when you get down to it do not dare get their hands dirty and so refuse to confront the real issues and the terrible problems that every revolution in the hungry world poses and demands, the issues and the problems that we Cubans are facing.

We have read what some of these weary, know-it-all, Yankee intellectuals have written about the Cuban revolution. The truth about them *is* simple: they have been hurt personally by their own past attempts to be political men in your country. And now they are living inside these old hurts, and they are blinded by them. It makes them live inside their own little hesitations and cruel fears, and at times grief, because they can make no real commitment.

Who are they to assume such a posture before the facts of our revolution in Cuba? By what miraculous insight do they *know* that it must end in terror and grief, as they suggest it will? When they come to Cuba, when they think about Cuba, they're not experiencing anything or anybody in Cuba. They are experiencing, once again, for the hundredth time, the failure of themselves as political men and as intellectuals.

A few of us were in school up there, back in the late forties and early fifties. We know how very easy it is to be a well-informed smart-aleck, loading up one's mind with sophisticated equivocations, with all the weary criticisms with the slightly tragic tone—all of it resting upon the collapsed dreams of the old disillusioned radicals. And no alternatives even considered, much less imagined, advanced, invented, demanded. They see the good, they see the bad, the yes, the no, the maybe—and they cannot take a stand. So instead they take up a tone. But they are never *in* it; they are just spectators.

And as spectators they are condescending, with such little reason to be; it does make us angry, and then furious at ourselves for allowing it to make us angry. We should, of course, ignore them; and yet, we keep thinking as we read, what has this spiritual hick ever done to earn such an air about our Cuban revolution? Has *he* ever acted? Has he ever taken his own life into his own hands? Much less, the much more serious—and morally perilous matter—has he ever by acting taken the lives of others, of many others, into his own hands? You can be sure of the answer—it is: Never.

But enough. In the showdown these days such people are just no good—for the hungry world. All they prove is the old joke: in the 1920's the world historical problem was, can there be "socialism in one country"? In the 1960's the world historical problem is, can there be "capitalism in one country"? And we don't think it's such a joke any more.

When we read what such people write, we can't help but think of the 250 students from all over the world—except for North America—who came to our first school city and worked alongside us in the building of it.

Well, anyway, that's something about our problem of education and culture and something your free intellectuals can do about it.

EIGHT

WHAT DOES "YANKEE" MEAN?

This is our last letter to you, unless you answer us. What we want most to say to you we can say best by asking you this question:

What does "Yankee" mean in the world today? What kind of people are you North Americans? We are asking you because in all truth, as we've said before, we simply do not understand you any more, if we ever did. We've been trying in these letters to explain ourselves to you. Won't you now try to explain yourselves to us? Of course, you'll have to do more than just talk, but first you'll have to do that. What is done and what is not done In Your Name about Cuba, is being watched by people all over the world. In it, these peoples see "the Yankee" revealing himself; when they read about Cuba and about the United States, they are reading about what "Yankee" means today.

Perhaps that isn't fair to you—whoever you are—but it's true, whether you know it or not. We've been assuming *you* haven't really known it.

And it's true whether you want it to be or not. We've been assuming that now you are going to welcome it. At least we think you ought to welcome it. Do you know why?

Because Cuba—listen, Yankee—Cuba is your big chance. It's your chance to establish once again what the United States perhaps once did mean to the world. It's your chance to make it clear how you're going to respond to all the chaos and tumult and glory, all the revolution and bloody mess and enormous hopes that are coming about among all the impoverished, disease-ridden, illiterate, hungry peoples of the world in which you, Yankee, are getting so fat and so drowsy.

151

|

We've been reading over copies of all the letters we've sent to you, and we want to make an apology. Now and then we've been carried away, what with our revolution and all, so we've been rude. Forgive us, won't you, Yankee? Despite everything, we really do like many of you we've really known—the official ones, we mean. We hope those that we've liked are "the real Yankees," although how can we know this? Nobody ever sees himself as others see him, and we've tried to explain in our very first letter why you and we have not really known each other.

But what we want to apologize for is that we've kept putting it to you how what "Yankees" have done and failed to do has caused us so much trouble. But, damn it, that's true. You must see that now. So now, we're afraid, we're going to be even more rude. First we're going to tell you what "Yankee" has meant and does mean to us; and then we're going to tell you what you ought to do about it. And the truth is, we don't really feel it's rude. We think it's the moment of truth about the Cuban revolution, for you.

It was the U.S. pressure, it was the U.S. propaganda, is was what the U.S. has failed to do in connection with our revolution that has forced us, finally, to see that maybe we do *belong* in the Soviet political alliance. But whether we "belonged" with them at first, and whether we "belong" with them now—what choice has your Government *ever* given us about this? And that's one thing "Yankee" means to us: no choices given.

At what point has your Government ever said to us: "Look, Cuban, we're very glad about your revolution. We're glad for the same reasons you are—because it's a way out of all the old horror you've lived with, all the poverty and exploitation and waste of Cuban resources and Cuban talent. We're glad because we do want Latin America really to be prosperous and really to be free. We know that for a long time some North American businesses have had a pretty good thing down there, but as a government we want you to know that we're going to cooperate with you—with the Government of Cuba. For we know your Government must now use all the resources of Cuba in some rational way for Cuba. And we're sure we can adjust the differences between you and these North American corporations of ours. If you run into trouble, please let us know and let us talk about it, will you?

"We want you to know that the meaning of 'Yankee' is not confined to what these corporations have done and are trying to do. After all, we North Americans *are* very rich, fabulously rich, and as a government and as a people we are not going to argue about the kind of money that's involved in Cuban investment. You see, we've given billions in aid to various countries, and we think that if the United States Government has to help Cuba pay for any economic damage the revolution does to this or to that private U.S. investment—well, that's the very best kind of aid we could possibly give. Because your revolution is the real thing, Cuban. We know that. Now, what can we do to help you make it a big economic and social and educational and political success?"

Did your Government *ever* say a single one of these sentences to us? The answer is no. And in the end, that's why we say now: *"Cuba, sí. Yankee, no!"* We can say "no" too, you see.

Moreover, please realize that the Russians *have* talked to us reasonably and with sanity, about tractors and oil and schools and sugar. So, please know too that we Cubans can also say "yes." After all, there are only two "worlds" today capable of really helping or really hurting us, capable of talking sane or insane.

What does "Yankee" mean? To us, so far, it means: Insane hurtfulness.

We're not against criticism! But anyone who is trying to help us instead of hurt us, must make his criticisms constructive. But what does that mean? First, that you tell us the reasons for your criticisms—not just voice your own hysteria. Second, that you try to point a way out, to suggest a policy, a plan, a program.

Some of the things about Cuba today which you may think are bad are quite plainly hangovers of the old order, not yet taken up and attended to by the revolution. Others, in all likelihood, are passing phases of the revolutionary process itself, inevitable features of the train of events, of upsurge, disorganization and attempted new beginnings. In either case, shouldn't you keep your mouth shut about them, except insofar as by understanding them you might help us to get past them?

Apart from hangovers of the old order, and passing circumstances attendant on the new beginnings, the things you find ambiguous or downright bad in Cuba today we think have in common certain peculiarities: most of them are features of *later* phases of the revolution. Many are due to international developments for which your Government itself is very much responsible. Many are due to Cuba's *old* international situation; they are results of those old relations standing in the way of our setting up a new Cuba. But most important to us: they are very much a part of what can only be called counterrevolutionary efforts that we must put down *if* the revolutionary gains are to be consolidated and the aims of the revolution pursued further. Surely, any of our critics should take all this into account.

But now we've reached a point where your Government probably can't say anything reasonable and sane to us. We certainly don't expect them to. Not any more. In fact, what we want from your Government and your monopolies can now be put into just one word: "Nothing." Or in four words: "Just let us *alone*."

II

But let us ask you this: *why* didn't your Government ever talk to us in the way we described above? It wouldn't have meant anything financially significant to you—to the citizens of the United States of America. Perhaps you have your own answer to this question. We don't know it, whatever it may be. Whatever your answer is, perhaps that's what "Yankee" means to you. But our belief is that the U.S. Government didn't talk reasonably to us, first, because those monopolies that "have had a pretty good thing down there" are telling your Government what to do. It's not your Government, and it's certainly not you, that is telling *them* what to do in countries like Cuba.

And second, we believe they didn't talk reasonably because it's not only Cuba, which, after all, from your standpoint is a small country with a small U.S. private investment. It's not only Cuba: it's all of Latin America and elsewhere too. As front men for all your monopolies in Latin America, your Department of State is thinking about all of Latin America, and they see quite well that if we Cubans take our own resources and our own talent and labor into our own hands and use them all for our own benefit, as any sovereign people must, then other Latin American countries might get the same fine idea. And do something about it, too.

That's why your Government was never reasonable and just and sane about our Cuban revolution. Or so we believe. Again—how many times have we asked it—if we are wrong, isn't it easy for you, who keep saying that you're the center of "the free world," isn't it easy for you to prove it to us? After all, we got much of the idea we've just expressed out of books that your own scholars have written about Latin America, as well as out of our own experience. Don't you ever read any of the true books about your own corporations and your own Government and your own military and how they are all tied up together all over the world today? And especially in Latin America? Since at least the beginning of the 20th century some of your best writers have been telling you about it.

All that, of course, is what we mean by "Yankee imperialism." It's not just a slogan; it's not just a shout; it's a big fact about your country and it's a big fact about the world today.

Perhaps the reason you don't really know about it, and we do, is because the big, sharp, brutal edges of Yankee imperialism don't show up yet inside the United States. They show up down here, and you're not down here. Down here is where it's brutal—just as all imperialism is brutal out on its own frontiers; it can afford to be gentle and nice in its home base, at least for a time.

But can it continue to be that way? We don't think that it really can. Do you know why?

Because we think Yankee imperialism is in the process of being defeated; as an economic system and as military garrisons all around the world and as a political apparatus—it is in the process of being defeated. It's in a deadly struggle, and the U.S. imperialists know this very well. They are not going to die without fighting. The more defeats they suffer, the more aggressive and the more stubborn they are going to become, the more loudly and ignorantly they are going to shout "communism!" at every real reform or revolution in the hungry world that they are exploiting, because each of these reforms and these revolutions means another defeat for them.

So as they are being defeated and come to realize it more and more, they're going to get into more and more of a panic. That is why we think that insofar as Cuba is concerned they will do their very best to make your Government make aggressions against us. Because our revolution is certainly a defeat for Yankee imperialism. That is why your head of state caused the O.A.S. to make meaningless proclamations against us.

We've already explained why they can't any longer do us real economic damage. So they are left with military aggression of some sort; that is all they've got left insofar as Cuba is concerned. Perhaps your Government is not such a fool as to attack us directly with the Marines and the paratroopers and the battleships. Although we're ready for that, too.

But can't *you* fight those imperialists? Perhaps you are still enough of a democracy at least to investigate their whole pressure system inside your economy and inside your Government and so try to stop them. Anyway, now that we've got the Russian offer of military protection against your Government, we think it more likely, as we've already told you, that Yankee military aggression will take the form of indirect action. Maybe they'll use mercenaries; maybe they'll try to assassinate our Fidel.

Oh, we know you don't believe that such things are possible; you don't really believe that your Government has got a CIA and an FBI and all the undercover "black" people around the world. But that's just another thing about Yankee imperialism you can't see and know about because, as yet, it's mainly part of the ugly edges out on the frontiers of the system that you are living under. You don't see it all up there, safe in the United States of America.

Even so, sometimes a tiny little glimpse of it does get into your newspapers—some rat you've hired defects or is caught; somebody gets murdered up a dark alley and it's hushed up quick.

We've read in your papers—so we don't know—that you can't, as a people, even investigate by your Congress exactly what all those Yankee spy outfits spend your money for. Is that true, Yankee? If it is, don't you see that it's a state within a state; and don't you see that with what's going on in the world today, it could very well mean enormous trouble and world disgrace for you? Don't you fear that as your imperialism is defeated and defeated, and as those who benefit by it, or are used by it, get into more and more of a panic—don't you fear that the ugly edges of it might be turned upon you also?

The road ahead is perilous not only for the hungry nations; the road is also perilous for the rich nations, and especially for the richest of them all. The rich imperialists of that richest nation of them all—they are not going to die without putting up a fight; and in the end, it will be a fight against you, as well as against us. What does "Yankee" mean? Maybe it is going to mean an hysterically anti-Communist, totalitarian state, the likes of which mankind has not yet known.

III

We don't think "Yankee imperialism" means that your State Department officials are necessarily in on the deals, as—say—the Batista politicians were in on the big-business deals in Cuba. What we do believe is that most U.S. officials, certainly those that have dealt with us, are living in a world so far removed from the realities of today that they really can't understand the what, the how, the when, and the why of any question of real significance. What they do more or less understand is largely irrelevant.

And what they understand least are their own worries —because they do not own up to the fear that is back of these worries: the fear that they are always going to be losing. And yet they don't even know what "losing" means. The ideals they proclaim *are* mere abstractions; they don't mean anything for the very same ideals when these ideals are made concrete, specific, and real by the thrust and drive of something like our Cuban revolution.

These officials of yours live in a different world, they are different *kinds* of men from us of the hungry world. We can understand something of them because we've been the weaker, and the weaker *have* to study the stronger, or they may be crushed by them. But they don't have the slightest glimpse of what we're really all about, and why, and what kinds of men and women we really are.

And most of them don't care, either. It's too much trouble. Besides, they'd have to learn Spanish, really learn it, and talk with us and read what we read. It's too much trouble. They would have really to "associate" with us, even if our skins were dark, and—Mother of God!—that would never do!

No, your foreign officials we've known are just not up to it all. They form an insulated little outpost of a curious kind of North American civilization, and in that little world they live. Because they are so insulated, they can't understand what is happening, and because they can't find out, they come to feel that they are superior people. We know that they feel this superiority: we know how they "try to be good fellows" with some of us. It's disgusting. Do they think we can't tell the difference between a human being and someone trying to put on an act as a human being?

They try first "to investigate us," to find out "who we really are." Then they make pleasant small chatter. Those are their ways of treating us: investigate cautiously, then be trivial.

Don't they know we want to talk sense about tractors and schools; and learn from the experience they've had in other parts of the world? But wherever they've been, what experiences have they really had? The same as they are having here? What else? Well, now we'll travel for ourselves in our own way and have our own experiences. We know how to be human beings—curious, open, flexible, eager to learn. We've already proven that, by the way we're making our revolution—and we're only beginning. Your officials, we think, they are through, most of them. They are part of a system that is being defeated, and inside themselves they are already defeated men.

IV

But what should you do?

We Cubans don't feel at all embarrassed about telling you what we think you ought to make your Government do. Often enough, it has told us what we Cubans ought to do, and made it stick, too. Besides, what you ought to do seems to us down here in Latin America so perfectly obvious, we just can't understand why you haven't already done it.

You ought to use Cuba as The Case—as The Case in which to establish the way you are going to act when there are revolutions in hungry countries everywhere in the world.

Whether you see it or not, that is how most people in the world are already seeing The Case of Cuba—as the real test of what "Yankee" means today. We Cubans think most of you Yankees these days are just wandering about, without aim, without knowing what's going on in the world, and in your own country, and without caring much. But you can't keep that up much longer. Aren't you beginning to realize that? You've got to act, because as we've told you, you are so powerful and you are so rich that for you to just do nothing, that *is* to act.

We know how hard it is to see things straight, and so to act right. We're in the middle of all these problems. But for you, especially, Yankee, it's going to be harder and harder, the way things are going, and the way you don't seem to be able to get real information about them. It's going to be harder and harder for you to distinguish between the real movements and sentiments of people, and what your newspapers *always* call "The Communist Conspiracies." The Russians, of course, are going to come out for any mass upsurge that occurs, and they are going to help it too, if only because it will be against you. So if you don't get smart, *they* are going to be "the defenders of the people" against your soldiers and your monopolists. We're not talking now about just the propaganda: because we've found out, and so have a lot of other people, that Russian oil and Czech machinery are just as good as any Yankee monopolists make or sell.

Well, Yankee, do you want soldiers and capitalists—and tourists, of course—do you want just them to represent you in the world? Is that now all that Yankee means? We don't know the answer for the whole world, but we are pretty sure about it for Cuba. That *is* the answer; that and not much else.

But only "so far." We are still hopeful, being revolutionaries ourselves. Let us not argue about the past. That is all over for Cuba. And let us not dwell further on the present; it's going to be changing very fast now. Let us suppose, hopefully, that you did wake up and so took Cuba as The Case. Then, how *should* you act? What should you do about the Cuba of the revolution? And about the Latin America of which we Cubans are now, for Yankee imperialists, such an annoying part?

You must first realize that what has happened and what is happening in Cuba is now central to all of America—North and South; that suddenly this small island of ours—this, in the phrase of our Fernando Ortiz, this "thick broth of civilization which bubbles on the Caribbean fire"—has become a major center of world affairs. Then you must realize that on the shores of Cuba the whole international posture of the United States of America has again collapsed in utter failure. Cuba is a dramatic specification of the general bankruptcy of U.S. policies and lack of policies, as your country fails to confront the hungry nations of the world, and as it confronts in such absurd ways the world initiative of the Soviet bloc.

Of course, nowadays, chaos and tumult, riots and rev-

olutions—against you—are breaking out all over. In particular they are breaking out all around the rim of the
Sino-Soviet bloc, which means: among the military outposts and the allies of the U.S.A. Nowadays, too, there's
always a crisis somewhere—for you—but now it is in
Cuba.

And Cuba is up close to the domain of the United
States. It's as close to the United States as is Taiwan or
Japan to Red China; as close as is Turkey or Afghanistan to the Soviet Union. And now the Soviet initiative
is *here*—not "contained" over there, in the Euro-Asiatic
hemisphere in which the United States has so ineffective-
ly tried to keep it. But surely there is no need for us to
relate to you in detail the chaos around the world and
the failure during the last decades of the United States
to confront it with reason and sanity.

So you must realize that your political leaders are not
responding to all this in any reasonable and effective way.
In fact, your political system itself doesn't seem capable
of responding in any way, except panic and wait-and-see
and hysteria, to the world hatred of which the United
States is becoming Target Number One. What, for example, has been the reaction to it all as revealed in your
1960 elections? Has either of your parties, your candidates for President of the United States of America, said
anything halfway adequate to the problems of the world
in which the United States now flounders? Are there any
debates about alternative policies, plans or programs
going on among you? What programs?

The answers are surely plain to anyone who can think.
The answers are all no. And that, in one word—no—is
one reason why we have been writing these letters to
you. Answer them, Yankee!

There's a Cuban problem—that is true. We have many
problems, and now these are mainly *our* problems. But
there is also a Washington and a Wall Street problem,
and these, they are your problems—aren't they, Yankee? But now you can't separate these problems—so
Latin America is your problem too, and Washington and
Wall Street and Latin American problems. That's how
it is between these two Americas.

Perhaps, given your condition, and the dead-end policies of your Government, you are thinking again, "Why not just go down there and beat hell out of them?" But surely you must know by now that you can't just send the Marines any more and get away with it. Those days are over. They are over because the people of Latin America just won't stand for it any more. They are over because Latin America is coming out of its centuries-long isolation from world history, and the peoples of the world just won't stand for it any more.

And there's another reason you can't just send the Marines: Russia. Whatever their motives, whatever they expect, we think it's true that the Russians *are* protecting us from you. Now we are very much a part of your cold war with them, and you can't take the risk of starting up a real war with Soviet missiles. We're sorry it took this kind of thing to free us from the fear of U.S. Marines landing again—if they did, it would be the fourth or fifth time—but there it is, Yankee.

One more thing that won't work: you must realize that no matter how rich you may be you can't just buy off people with your money any more. It's true you can buy up some ruling generals and land owners with "aid" —most of your aid so far has been military, you know. But you can't buy off the peoples of Latin America. For one thing, these peoples know that what some of your politicians now call "A Marshall Plan for Latin America" —if anything comes of it—is mainly due to our Cuban revolution; they know it's due to your fear that we've become the trigger for all the guns in Latin America. But, you see, we *are* just the vanguard, even in this respect: even in getting money from the United States Government for other Latin American countries. And these countries know that. It's perfectly obvious to them that your Government's offers of increased aid to them —and nobody has seen much money, yet—is due to what we've done and what we're doing; it is due to the success of our Cuban revolution.

It is also due to the success of the Soviet bloc as a whole. You want less to help us in Latin America than to hurt them, the Russians—"to contain them." Only a few years ago, you were "containing" them in Asia and Europe; now you're "containing" them in Latin America.

Well, we Latin Americans will welcome any aid we can get, because, of course, we do need it. But we are going to take it on our own terms or not at all. Remember, you *are* in a world competition, and we've already found that the strings attached by your Russian and Chinese competitors, whatever they may turn out to be, are *not* imperialistic strings. The fact is, so far, there are very few strings of any kind attached to our commercial transactions with them. And it is a kind of transaction that does help us do exactly what we want to do, and what must be done: to make our country truly independent and sovereign, economically as well as politically. So violence and cash, they are no longer the answers.

V

What you must do, we think, is to act politically inside your own country to insure that your Government will not use violence, directly or indirectly, in any form, against the Cuban revolution.

Hands off Cuba!

That, in three words, is what we want above all else from you. Is that too much to ask? If we were really sure of that, the new nation we're giving birth to would be enormously relieved, and the pains of its birth would be enormously lessened. It would greatly increase our chances to work out well all the political and cultural worries we've been so frank about with you in these letters.

So: get your Government to leave us alone.

But to do that you must get your Government truly to acknowledge once and for all that Cuba is a sovereign state, and you must make your Government realize what that means, and act on the realization. It means that you can't say: We Yankees "bar a Red Cuba" or any other kind of Cuba. To say such things—and your very own President has said it—is surely both arrogant and

silly. You are not our policemen, much less our government. To acknowledge our sovereignty means that whatever kind of government and whatever kind of economy
we set up inside Cuba is not subject to *any* orders,
on any subject, from Washington or Wall Street, or from
anywhere else outside Cuba. It means that on an equal
footing and with mutual respect, the Government of
Cuba and the Government of the United States talk
over reasonably whatever differences they may have.
It means that your Government give up, once and for
all, the absurd and hysterical idea that they can destroy
what our revolution means.

Our revolutionary Government, under that one condition, is perfectly willing, we always have been willing,
to negotiate with your Government such questions as the
forms and the means of payment for the Yankee properties we have taken for our own use, and the whole
question of the foreign commerce between the United
States and Cuba.

But there is more to it than just creating good will
between governments. There is the fact of these U.S.
corporations and how they do business in Latin America
and how they are tied up with existing Latin American
governments.

The United States cannot "export" skill and capital
by means of many of the existing governments of Latin
America. The U.S. must help create capital and skill
down here, in all these countries: we must create our
own skill and our own capital. That is what we Cubans
have done and are doing. And this means that if your
Government doesn't support such revolutions as ours, at
least they must not act against them.

But here's your problem: they cannot do this because
all the revolutions of consequence will be economically
against the Yankee monopolies—and so also, politically,
against the Yankee Government. They will be politically
nationalist, and economically they will be against the
United States corporations operating abroad. That is
why, the way things are, if we Cubans win, the U.S. Government as it now exists and the U.S. big-business oli-
garchy as it now exists—they are going to lose.

Therefore, isn't it clear? If you want to act with reference to Cuba and all "the Cubas" that are going to occur, you've first got to act in your own country. You've got to talk to your own Government and you've got to get your Government to do something about the big Yankee monopolies that "operate"—a good word—in Latin America.

Now we're getting down to your real problem; we hope you see that. You're coming up against the economic and political structure of the United States of America.

So it seems to us, you're up against this: You've got to make your Government change its whole line of policy; you've got to argue for a completely new United States approach to the problems of the hungry world.

But to do that you've got to change drastically the whole economic system of your big corporations, at least as they operate outside the U.S.A.

You've got to smash Yankee imperialism from inside the United States. For you can't hope to make your Government—if it is your Government—change its line of policy unless you do smash that system. That is, not unless the North American imperialists act as no commanding class has ever acted before. And perhaps that is asking too much of them. Besides, maybe not enough of you North Americans care, and too many of your politicians in charge of things are too blind and too fat.

That is why by their actions, they are making our own revolution become harder, and are hampering the development of our economy, and of our political system of a new and possibly daringly democratic sort.

That is why, from their point of view, the basic view upon which U.S. policy has so far been based, the answer to the question—"What should the U.S. do?"—is: It can now do nothing much of any consequence, except military invasion, direct or indirect, of our Cuba.

That is why, if they are to act at all, short of military action, the U.S. must first change its policy line: basing their new policy upon one fact—the acceptance of the Cuban revolution. But to do that, the U.S. Government would have to transform its own imperialist economy.

Without that, we Latin Americans cannot expect any-thing from the Yankees, and so we do not expect any-thing, except more grief and trouble. It would have to be a deep transformation: the United States corporations would have to stop being exporters of capital which they continue to own. There you find the reasons for all the problems. The United States would have to send capital out of the United States not as owners, but as lenders, to help the underdeveloped countries, not to buy them up. Your Government would have to make those cor-porations renounce the ownership of the riches of our countries. You Yankees would have to use your own riches, which are surely great enough. In fact, any ra-tional use of the resources of the United States would permit you an infinite development, and at the same time you could help mightily other countries. But of course that is mainly your concern, or we hope it is.

But what *is* our concern is the fact that there cannot be peace—by which we mean real understanding—be-tween North and South America as long as these Yankee corporations own the riches of our countries. Because with that kind of ownership goes the real control of the politics of our countries. The ownership of our riches means the control of our politics. That's not ideology. That's just a plain fact that we have lived in Cuba and that most of Latin America is still living.

VI

We Cuban revolutionaries don't really know just ex-actly *how* you could best go about this transforming of your Yankee imperialism. For us, with our problems, it was simple: In Cuba, we had to take to our "Rocky Mountains"—you couldn't do that, could you? Not yet, we suppose.

(We're joking—we suppose. But if in ten years, in five years—if things go as we think they might inside your country, if it comes to that, then know this, Yan-kee: some of us will be with you. God almighty, those are great mountains!)

But for you, with your problems, we can see that it's

not very simple; certainly it wouldn't be easy. But you're a democracy, aren't you? Your politicians keep saying you are. And you Yankees are a vigorous people, or at least once upon a time you were. And you are now in a position almost nobody else in the world is now in, not yet:

Because you are so rich and so powerful, you are in a position to decide what you are going to do with your life and with your country. Your real alternatives are big alternatives. *That* is why you are still a frontier. You could really ask *how* men should live; you're not tied down to the struggle just to exist. Yes, you're still on a frontier, Yankee, if you want to be. And the frontier for you—don't you see it?—first of all, it's down here to your South, and over to your East. It's the hungry world, Yankee, the world of Latin America, of Africa, of Asia. But, first of all, perhaps, it's got to be inside the U.S. political economy.

If you'd just forget the money—Mother of God, haven't you already enough?

If you'd just abandon the fear—aren't you strong enough to?

If you'd just stop being so altogether private and become public men and women of the world—you could do great things in the world: as a people, as an individual, as a government. As you might say: You could make it, Yankee.

Well, forgive us, friend. It's your life, not ours; it's your country, not ours. We've got our own lives to live, and we're going to live them as best we can. And *now* we've got our own country, too, and it's going to stay ours from now on. We've done enough fighting for both these rights—to live our own lives and to live it in our own country. And plenty of work, too. So have you, Yankee—once upon a time. But what are you going to do *now*? And what do you think the U.S.A. should do *now*—that's what we Cubans are wondering.

And yet—hear us well, Yankee—we're almost through —the question is not really:

"What should the United States do?"

The real question is: "Who or what *is* the United States today?"

What does "Yankee" mean? Who or what is going to decide how your enormous powers are going to be used, as they come to bear upon our Cuba? And upon all the peoples of the hungry world? The State Department? The sugar interests? The Kremlin? The Pentagon? The oil companies?

Yankee imperialism or the people of North America?

Listen, Yankee: we Cubans don't know the answers to these questions. Do you—whoever you are? But one thing we do know: in one way or another, from now on and insofar as Cuba is concerned, we Cubans are going to be in on those decisions.

So—goodbye, Yankee.

We Cubans, we are waiting for your answer.

Goodbye, Yankee. You're on your own now.

NOTE TO THE READER, II

The major purpose of this book, as I have explained in my first note to the reader, is to discover the full argument of the Cuban revolutionary and to state it as accurately as I am able. Having now done this, I feel the need to comment briefly on this Cuban voice to which we have been listening. It is a dangerous need—for me at least: It could so easily lead to the writing of another book—on "Cuba, Latin America and the United States." Perhaps later. But for the present, I feel it urgent that the Cuban voice be heard—now. So I must comment, but I must keep my comment brief.

Let me say at once that the Cuban argument presented in these pages, I find on the whole compelling. It does not seem to me very useful to take up each point in it, expressing agreement or disagreement: That is for the reader to do. Parts of it I feel to be much stronger than others: And those parts which worry me most are what also worry many of those whom I believe to be among the most intelligent—and it happens, the most powerful—of the Cuban revolutionaries. But generally, I find their argument persuasive. To explain why, I must first state something of what I have come to believe about Latin America in general today.

I

Latin America is enormously rich—in soil, timber, oil, all the metals, the chemicals; it is rich in virtually everything men need to live well. Yet in this plundered continent there exist today some of the most hopelessly impoverished and most consistently exploited people in the world.

Most of these countries—like the old Cuba—are one-crop economies, and thus dependent upon the fluctuations of world prices and the impersonal calculations of foreign bankers.

Most of these countries—like the old Cuba—are, in fact, run by an alliance of foreign capital and local interests of the most retrograde character it is possible to imagine. Most of their governments—like the old Cuba's —are a world joke on the meaning of "constitutional democracy." In this part of the world, governments tend to be branches of private enterprise; "democracy" in much of Latin America is largely a façade tolerated by an army, a ceremony displayed on due occasion.

In many of these countries—like the old Cuba—no real reforms can be undertaken without the approval of The Military, whose take of the national budgets runs well above 20%. Only in Mexico in 1914, in Bolivia in 1952, and in Cuba in 1958–59, have regular armies been smashed by revolution; and *only* in these three countries has there been any attempt really to deal with the basic problems of land.

There is, of course, considerable variety; each country has its own problems as well as those peculiar to this world region. Brazil, for example, has for four years been undergoing a capitalist boom. It is a "dual society": there is the capitalist-rich Sao Paulo area, with its urban population caught in an inflationary wage-price squeeze; and there is the rest, an internal colony. Perhaps half the population is not in any money economy at all; and in the impoverished northeast, at times, people live off cactus. Brazil is in itself a continent—and a curiously colonial power.

In the six "republics" of Central America, a few hundred elite families own most of the land; a middle class scarcely exists; the immense majority live in drudgery, poverty, sloth; more than half are illiterate. Bananas in Honduras and Panama; cotton in Nicaragua; coffee and bananas in Costa Rica; in the others, coffee—these are the "dessert" export crops around which these economies revolve.

Argentina continues to do nothing of significance to develop its real wealth—land, cattle, grain; three fourths of her people live in the cities, most of them underemployed; industry is stagnant, inflation is continuing, the Government is more and more dependent upon the army. Meanwhile armed men are in the pampas—the finest farmland in Latin America; police terror is frequent in the cities.

Chile, officially embracing the cherished principles of political democracy and free-enterprise capitalism, is getting into hock to financial agencies dominated by the United States. These agencies provide small loans and in return dictate financial policies to a conservative government. One fourth of the population is an inflated white-collar throng. And again, there is utter neglect of the land: Some 86% of it is held in large *fundos,* the owners of which are more interested in profitable speculation in land than in farming it. In Chile, the farming is bad; in Chile, traditional poverty is institutionalized; in Chile, some one third of the men are drunk every week end—and perhaps 60% of the lower classes.

Probably three fourths of the inhabitants of Peru exist outside any money economy, waiting hopelessly on the edge of starvation (average daily caloric intake: 1,900). Sulphur fumes from the copper smelters blanket the wet mountains; the mining towns are not habitations for human beings, but human beings do exist there. And Peru, we are assured, is a highly constitutional democracy.

The recent history of Venezuela is one of economic madness. Professor Edwin Lieuwen states that when the dictator Gomez died in 1935, "an economic dictator had already inherited Venezuela . . . the petroleum industry was the new ruler. The new tyrant was immortal, and political upheavals disturbed it little. It answered only to the demands of the market in the United States and in western Europe and waited for the signals to be called from abroad." Oil accounts for over 90% of Venezuela's foreign income, provides 63% of her Government revenues, but employs only 3% of her labor force. So far as industrial development is concerned, the petroleum industry has led to what the Mexican economist Edmundo Flores calls "a chromeplated dead-end." The constitutionally elected president, Betancourt, has today inherited the consequences of this economic madness which, according to Paul Johnson, includes: "the highest cost economy in the world, which is driving Venezuelan oil out of the world market; seven different police forces; a huge, over-paid bureaucracy; inflated armed forces equipped with expensive gadgets like supersonic fighters [a nuclear submarine is on order] and a great sheaf of unpaid bills." In the meantime, President Betancourt has been "forced to turn to the U.S. for loans, with all that this entails in social and economic stagnation. Basic land reform has been shelved . . . unemployment is swelling. The growing anger of the mob [of the unemployed of Caracas] can be balanced only by more concessions to the army."

And Mexico? Her great revolution of 1910 and the following years has stalled. In a word, a revolution that began with the demand for land and for liberty seems to be ending in a plutocracy sitting within their state and on top of a capitalist economy—and full of revolutionary rhetoric. The old revolutionaries have become enriched political capitalists. To them, as well as to the newly made middle classes, "revolution" has been and is a highly profitable business—in recent years, 1% of the population has gotten as much as 51% of the national income—yet the governing classes all talk ultra-Left.

The Mexican revolutionaries have long memories: They know that "tourism" alone contributes almost one fourth of their country's foreign-exchange earnings, yet they do not forget that a hundred years ago the United States took by force an enormous chunk of Mexico's national territory. They know well that there is no progressive tax on personal income—but also they remember all about their fight with the United States, only yesterday, when they took their own oil resources into their own hands. They may be old and rich—but they know all about the use of Catholicism in counterrevolutions.

Nowadays, in Mexico, students are demonstrating— against the Yankee; and unlike the United States, Mexico is not monolithic on the question of Cuba. Mexico is split. Even the old revolutionaries see in Fidel Castro something of their own lost youth. The wind that once swept Mexico may yet sweep it again. Despite everything, which today is quite a lot, Mexico is a windy place.

Latin America is a great world region; it is a continent, long and repeatedly plundered; and it is in revolutionary ferment. That it is now in such ferment is a heartening testimony to the will of man not to remain forever an exploited object. For over a century Latin American man has been largely outside world history—except as an object; now he is entering that history—as a subject, with vengeance, with pride, with violence. The unilateral Monroe Doctrine is part of the epoch of Latin American isolation: it is isolationism on a hemispheric scale, and a shield for U.S. exploitation. That epoch, and with it the Monroe Doctrine, is now coming to an end.

But isn't there another side to it? Of course. Latin America *is* a continent, and as such it is various. Convictions about it are as sharply divided as they are passionately held.[1] But insofar as it is possible to describe the general scene in brief, we must pay attention to:

The unbelievable poverty (perhaps two thirds of these people are undernourished); the ill-health (about one half of these people have infectious or deficiency diseases); the illiteracy (about one half); the internal colonies (some one third of these people are outside the Latin American economic and cultural community); the steady exploitation (two thirds of these people are in semifeudal conditions of work); the one-crop export economies (and so the perilous dependence upon the fluctuations of foreign markets); the unjust and inefficient systems of land ownership and tenure (two thirds of the land is controlled—and often misused—by native oligarchies and foreign corporations); the foreign domination (perhaps a majority of the "extractive industries" is owned or controlled by foreign capital); the inadequate transportation systems (what exist are mainly means of transporting raw materials from inland to coast,

---

1 The best statements of "a more hopeful view" are based upon expectations about the political role of the middle classes. Of these statements, probably the best is by John J. Johnson, *Political Change in Latin America* (Stanford University Press, 1958). Although I do not agree with Professor Johnson's assessment of the "middle sectors," nevertheless, I think his book "indispensable reading" for anyone who wishes to understand the Latin American scene.

rather than means suitable for the development of internal markets); the ineffective credit systems and the lack of any real trade within and between these countries themselves (trade between them runs to about 7% of the world trade of Latin America); the repeated interventions—commercial and military—by great world powers; the political domination by feudal oligarchies, mixed with foreign corporate interests, and subject to the arbitrary actions of inflated armies: The Military Arbiters. (Since the end of the Second World War, governments of Latin America have "changed hands" without regard to "formal procedures" at least 31 times.)

Such are the salient realities of Latin America—yesterday and today.

Yesterday—but not today—they were the realities of Cuba.

II

The second general fact it is necessary to understand is the role the United States has played and is playing inside Latin America. This role I have already indicated: the "foreign capital" involved is largely U.S. capital; the aid given to the local armies, and hence in support of the feudal oligarchies, is U.S. aid. Inside Latin America, the U.S. Government has supported reactionary circles and do-nothing ruling strata. Its role has generally been and continues to be that of stabilizing their domination and so the continued sloth. Its aid has been largely to give *them* arms and other military support, in the name of "Hemispheric Defense," which has meant defense against their own people.

About this "aid": Since the end of World War II, the U.S. has given in direct aid about 31 *billion* dollars to countries outside Latin America, and only some 625 *million* dollars to Latin America—less than to the Philippines alone. For its "loans" (which have amounted to some 2.5 billion), the U.S. exacts acceptance of economic policies which, given the declining prices of Latin American commodities, cancel out all aid and loans. "During the last ten years," Paul Johnson sums it up, "the collapse of world commodity prices (from which the U.S. along with the other advanced industrial countries, has drawn immense benefit) has meant a net reduction in the income of Latin-America of over 1,000 million a year—three times as much, in aggregate, as the sum total of aid and loans the area has received during the same period. This is the brutal arithmetic which explains why tens, perhaps hundreds, of millions of Latin-Americans, poor as they are, are getting steadily poorer."

"Preachments," A. 'A. Berle Jr. recently remarked, "about the value of private enterprise and investment and the usefulness of foreign capital were, to most students of the situation, a little silly. . . . Probably if the truth were known, this form of economic development in Latin America at the moment is a minority rather than a majority function. . . . Foreign aid or private investment may industrialize, may increase production, and still leave the masses in as bad shape as ever."

U.S. trade with Latin America is, of course, larger than U.S. trade with any other world region; U.S. investment in Latin America, amounting now to about 9 billion dollars, is larger than U.S. investment in any other region of the world. Mining properties and oil are the largest elements in this investment, and both are needed by the U.S. economy as it is now operated. Accordingly: the job of the U.S. Government has been to promote trade and to protect investment. In pursuance of these aims, the official line has been to maintain political stability among the dominated, irrespective of forms of government, in order that business might continue as usual. The rest is oratorical embellishment—perhaps needed to insure the votes of these governments in the U.N. That, in a few sentences, seems to me the essential truth of the matter.

But there is more to it: The U.S. has supplied arms to all 20 of these countries, and to 12 of them has made grants of military aid; it has set up Military Missions, which, in the opinion of Professor Lieuwen—author of the most balanced and comprehensive account of the matter—have "no genuine military objective." The official rationale given for all this is fear of Communist aggression. But: In any real East-West fight, the kind of arms provided seem quite irrelevant; and the Communist parties inside Latin America are not only generally weak but clearly grow on the deplorable economic and social conditions which these U.S. policies help to insure. Regardless of the sincerity of official intentions, the real functions of such military aid have been persuasively stated by Professor Lieuwen: In most of these countries the armed forces "play key political roles" and are "seemingly insatiable" in their desire for arms. "Thus military training and assistance are provided to secure—and to insure—political cooperation. . . . Political gains [to the U.S.] are expected to flow from the military programs: well-disposed governments, support for U.S. policies in international organizations, and assurance of access to military bases and strategic raw materials in Latin America. A further objective of the military programs is to promote political stability in this low-priority area so that our maximum energies can be devoted elsewhere. The simple reasoning is that the better the army in any Latin American republic, the less likely that internal order will be subverted."

That more democratic *forms* of government have come about in several Latin American countries since the end of World War II—Mr. A. A. Berle Jr. states—has "been treated by the Department of State as an almost trivial change—and not a wholly agreeable one." (Perhaps the Department has been sound in its judgment of the triviality of the change.) Mr. Berle adds that in the past, the State Department has carried on its friendship with "dictators" who have had "to maintain a steady and frequently an increasingly cruel policy of suppressing popular opposition by police methods [but] the United States took pains not to show sympathy with their opponents—irrespective of the quality of the men or of the forces they symbolized. In this attitude, the Department was supported by a steady stream of reports from the chiefs of dictatorial secret police to the effect that all their opponents were 'Communist.' This material found its way into the State Department files, and was fed to Congressional and other officials. It proved a useful excuse for harrying and harassing entirely genuine democratic leaders and movements. . . . Whether in their own countries, or in exile or refuge in the United States, the democratic leaders found themselves baffled, discredited, almost persecuted by the Government of the United States—supposedly the symbol of democracy."

Is it any wonder, then, that in the minds of many intelligent Latin Americans, the United States of America more often than not stands for political tyranny, economic exploitation, continued impoverishment, and military domination? Is it any wonder that Mr. Nixon was spit upon during his attempt to make a good-will tour? That it was a surprise to most North Americans reveals the inadequacy of the North American press: It was a reflection of everyday realities in Latin America.

"The sad truth," write Professors Pike and Bray, "is that the state of affairs in Latin America has sunk to the level that the United States could help to destroy a democratic regime by 'embracing' it." In one respect at least, the United States in the 20th century stands in the same relationship to Latin America as Czarist Russia in the 19th century stood to Europe: The U.S.A. is a reactionary menace to any real attempt to modify the basic realities of Latin America. Generally, whenever in Latin America people have really begun to get on the move, in the face of their movement the policies and the lack of policies of the United States have been consistently counterrevolutionary.

Certainly that has been and certainly that is the case in connection with the revolution in Cuba.

III

In the general context of Latin America and in terms of the role in Latin America of the United States, the Cuban revolution is a new phenomenon. Some of its features have been available elsewhere, at one time or another, but the specific Cuban combination is historically unique.

1: Like Mexico's revolution of 40 years ago, Cuba's is based upon the peasantry, but the land reform in Cuba is far more thorough, rapid, and successful than Mexico's or Bolivia's. (In many recent years, Mexico has still had to import footstuffs.) Elsewhere, there is no significant land reform.

2: In at least six Latin American nations, the vicious role of the traditional military apparatus in political, social and economic life has been destroyed. In Cuba, this apparatus has been totally and almost suddenly smashed—and with it the dominant economic powers.

3: The Cuban revolution has swiftly destroyed the economic basis of capitalism—both foreign and Cuban. Most of this power was foreign—in fact, North American. It has now been destroyed with a thoroughness unique in Latin American history.

4: Moreover, Cuba's economic success—due primarily to her successful and intelligent agrarian reform, and helped at a decisive juncture by her economic agreements and trading with Soviet-bloc countries—makes Cuba impregnable to effective economic blockade or pressure from U.S. interests.

There are, of course, other features of this revolution, but it is this combination that is unique in Latin America. And it is this combination, with various modifications and additions, that in my judgment is now a major alternative to continued misery elsewhere in Latin America. One thing that might stop it from becoming the most probable alternative is a drastic change in U.S. policy. But given the character of the political economy of the U.S. today, I do not think it reasonable to expect a change of the sort that would be needed: The United States Government would have to actively help Latin Americans destroy the vested interests inside their own countries as well as the vested interests of U.S. corporations now operating in these countries. For it is this alliance of U.S. capital with local interests that now rules much of Latin America today—and so helps to keep it in the condition that it is in.

Without the destruction of these interests—both Latin and North American—no real economic changes can reasonably be expected, certainly not at a sufficiently rapid rate. And without such structural economic changes, "democracy" will remain what it now is in most of this continent: A farce, a fraud, a ceremony.

IV

And that is why I am for the Cuban revolution. I do not worry about it, I worry for it and with it. Like most Cubans, I too believe that this revolution is a moment of truth, and like some Cuban revolutionaries, I too believe that such truth, like all revolutionary truth, is perilous.

Any moment of such military and economic truth *might* become an epoch of political and cultural lies. It *might* harden into any one of several kinds of dictatorial tyranny. But I do not believe that this is at all inevitable in Cuba. And I do believe that should it happen it would be due, in very large part, to the role the Government of the United States has been and is continuing to play in Cuban affairs.

Were I a Cuban, I have no doubt that I would be working with all my effort for the success of my revolution. But I am not a Cuban. I am a Yankee. To me, this does not mean that I am any the less "for" their revolution. For, like L. T. Hobhouse, whose creed at this point, I share,[2] I cannot give unconditional loyalties to any institution, man, state, movement or nation. My loyalties are conditional upon my own convictions and my own values. And in this matter, both of these lie more with the Cuban revolution than with the official United States reaction to it.

The policies the United States has pursued and is pursuing against Cuba are based upon a profound ignorance, and are shot through with hysteria. I believe that if they are continued they will result in more disgrace and more disaster for the image of my country before Cuba, before Latin America, and before the world.

Moreover, I think that U.S. policies and lack of policies are very real factors in *forcing* the Government of Cuba to align itself politically with the Soviet bloc, as against assuming a genuinely neutralist and hence peaceful world orientation. In fact, these policies are making it

[2] L. T. Hobhouse, *Liberalism* (London: Oxford University Press, 1911).

very difficult indeed for Cubans even to discuss such an orientation. More than any other single factor, these U.S. policies are forcing the Cuban Government to become "harder," to become more restrictive of freedom of expression inside Cuba. In brief, they are forcing Cubans to identify all "minority views" with "counterrevolution." And they are forcing the Cuban Government to identify "anticommunism" with "counterrevolution."

Let me say, as flatly as I am able to say, that were I a Cuban, acting in the Cuban revolution today, I too should feel it necessary to make this latter identification. For the plain truth is that the kind of ignorant and hysterical "anticommunism" that is now the mood, the tone, and the view of many of the highest governmental officials of the United States of America *is* of the McCarthy type. And I am just as opposed to this as I am to Stalinist practice and proclamation. Surely our aim, in the U.S.A. and in the U.S.S.R., should be to go beyond both.

The Cuban Government, as of mid-1960, is *not* "Communist" in any of the senses legitimately given to this word. The Communist Party of Cuba, as a party, does *not* pose any serious threat to Cuba's political future. The leading men of Cuba's Government are not "Communist," or even Communist-type, as I have experienced communism in Latin America and in research work in the Soviet Union. On all these counts, I find the Cuban argument, as presented in letter number five, generally convincing.

It is worth examining the evidence presented by North American writers of the contrary opinion, for to do so, I believe, is to reveal its weakness. In his article in the October 1960 issue of *Foreign Affairs*, Mr. A. A. Berle Jr. gives three grounds for his identification of "Cuba" with "Communism":

1: "When Batista fell," Mr. Berle writes, "the hard-core Communist cadres found little, if any, choate force to prevent them from taking over."

This *assumes* that these "hard-core Communist cadres" are necessarily efficient, in contrast to the non-Communist revolutionaries who *made* the revolution against, it so happens, Communist-Party opposition;[3] it assumes that such revolutionaries have been incapable of creating or of being a "choate force." I think both assumptions very dubious, and I would ask: Has Mr. Berle spent as much as one week in any one INRA zone observing what is going on insofar as personnel is concerned?

2: The second ground for his assumption which Mr. Berle gives is that the defectors from the revolution have stated as their reason for defection that the regime is "Communist." Given the context of their defection— the United States—it would surely be unreasonable to expect them to give any other reason. At any rate, I am certainly not willing, as Mr. Berle presumably is, to take the assertions of these men as either knowledgeable or detached evidence on this important historical matter.

3: The only other ground I find in his essay, Mr. Berle puts in this way: "The undeniable fact is that in result its orientation became, in terms of foreign relations as well as in terms of structure, Communist in character."

In terms of foreign relations: Does it make a government Communist if it trades with the Soviet bloc? If so, many countries indeed are suddenly made "Communist." Does it make a government Communist if it feels itself, rightly or wrongly, to be menaced militarily by a non-Communist country, and so accepts the Soviet Union's protection *on condition* that it *is* invaded? There is, to be sure, room for argument on these questions, but their answers may not merely be assumed. Moreover, the "foreign relations" of Cuba are, as yet, by no means frozen, as Mr. Berle generally assumes.

As for "structure," surely one must ask Mr. Berle to be a little more precise. "Communism" in the world today is neither homogeneous nor unchanging. Cuba's economic structure is certainly not Stalinist. Does Mr. Berle refer to Bolshevism in 1920? To Yugoslavia in 1950? To Khrushchev's Russia today? To Mao's China? Well, what *does* Mr. Berle mean by "Communist"?

The Cuban revolutionary *is* a new and distinct type of

[3] See Theodore Draper's article, cited in the notes—the most careful historical account I have seen in the American press.

left-wing thinker and actor. He is neither capitalist nor Communist. He is socialist in a manner, I believe, both practical and humane. And if Cuba is let alone, I believe that Cubans have a good chance to keep the socialist society they are building practical and humane. If Cubans are properly helped—economically, technically and culturally—I believe they would have a *very* good chance.

I do not agree with this black-or-white thinking of Mr. Berle and many others. I agree with Professor Antonio García of Colombia that Latin America need be subservient neither to the U.S.A. nor the U.S.S.R., and that the essence of U.S. policy has been "to fight Communism with merely political and military means" — to which I would add: and with the most inadvisable identification of everything not in line with the capitalist world as "communism." Such an identification makes the formulation of a cogent foreign policy toward the hungry-nation bloc next to impossible.

V

My worries for Cuba—like those of knowledgeable Cuban revolutionaries—have to do, first, with problems of politics. The Government of Cuba is a revolutionary dictatorship of the peasants and workers of Cuba. It is legally arbitrary. It is legitimized by the enthusiastic support of an overwhelming majority of the people of Cuba. Each of these three facts about it must be recognized, as well as that Professors Pike and Bray are surely correct in their statement that "the formalistic shell of the American way of life was exportable to nineteenth-century Latin America. It is not today."

I do not like such dependence upon one man as exists in Cuba today, nor the virtually absolute power that this one man possesses. Yet I believe it is not enough either to approve or to disapprove this fact about Cuba. That is much too easy; it is also politically fruitless. One must understand the conditions that have made it so, and that are continuing to make it so; for only then can one consider the prospects of its development. The conditions for the present political facts in Cuba seem to me to be ex-

pressed as well as they can be by the Cubans in letter
six. I believe that the revolutionary politics of Cuba are
part of a phase, and that I and other North Americans
should help the Cubans pass *through* it.

Moreover, the character and the actions of the man
in question, Fidel Castro, are not irrelevant to the probable outcome. In my judgment, one must take seriously
this man's own attempts to shift roles, even in the middle
of his necessary action, and his own astute awareness of
the need to develop a more systematic relation between
a government of law and the people of Cuba. In this,
again, he is acting under great difficulties, many of which
are due to the policies and the defaults of the Government of the United States.

As for elections in Cuba today: I share the view of
every competent observer that in any election the victory of the *Fidelistas* would be overwhelming. But what
seems to me more relevant to the question is that no
matter how an election were organized, and no matter
how it might be supervised by any international agency,
such a victory would be quite meaningless. To have
meaningful elections it is necessary to have at least two
political parties and it would be necessary for these parties to campaign on some range of issues. The only issue
in Cuba today is the revolution, conceived by the Cuban
Government primarily as economic and educational construction and as the military defense of Cuba's sovereignty. Any party that campaigned in Cuba today against
the revolution and against the present Government's
management of it would probably be set upon by the
majority of the people of Cuba. So I think it must be
faced up to: a real election in Cuba today is an impossible and meaningless idea. It could only be made meaningful by deliberately giving institutional form to the
counterrevolution, and that today would not be acceptable to the immense majority of the people of Cuba.

The absence of elections signifies the "absence of
democracy" only on the formal assumption that the electoral process is at all times and in all places indispensable
to democracy. But be that as it may, an election in Cuba

is at the present time an impossible and a meaningless demand.

In the meantime North Americans may as well realize that their own recent elections have certainly not been effective advertisements for the virtue or the necessity of the U.S. type of electoral process. To many intelligent Latin Americans, as well as to other nations of the hungry-nation bloc, they have seemed a race between two parties which differ little if at all on any real issues. To Cubans, they have also seemed a competition in belligerent ignorance about their country, rather than any reasonable public debate about actual problems Cubans— and the world—must now confront.

VI

The real political issue of Cuba and in Cuba seems to me to be this: Is it possible by revolutionary means of the sort being used in Cuba to build a genuinely free society? Is it possible to carry through in such drastic and rapid ways a revolution as fundamental as this one without producing either revolutionary terror or permanent dictatorship?

To my mind, these are not simple or unambiguous questions. How can they be, when the very meaning of "free society" is certainly quite open to debate? But I am unwilling—as are the Cuban revolutionaries—to identify "free society" only with the forms and mechanisms that have been historically developed in the United States or in various nations of Western Europe.

The historical record of the political outcomes of past revolutions is also ambiguous, but on the whole I think it leads one to pessimistic conclusions insofar as freedom is immediately concerned. The question is: Under what conditions can the Cuban revolution be different? No one can now truly answer this question. But let us consider briefly one comparison: Bolshevik Russia in about 1920 and Cuba today.

The internal situation of the Cuban Government is almost the precise opposite to that of the early Bolshevik Government. After a short visit to Russia, Bertrand Russell wrote in 1920: "The Government represents the interests of the urban and industrial population, and is, as it were, encamped amid a peasant nation, with whom its relations are rather diplomatic and military than governmental in the ordinary sense. . . . If Russia were governed democratically, according to the will of the majority, the inhabitants of Moscow and Petrograd would die of starvation." [4]

In contrast, Cuba's Government today represents, above all, the interests of the people of the countryside, and moreover, it has managed to balance quite well these interests with those of the urban wage worker. There is no problem of food, which in the Russia of 1920 was indeed a terrible problem. The Cuban revolution, unlike the Russian, has, in my judgment, solved the major problems of agricultural production by its agrarian reform.

The early Soviet Government was under effective economic blockade: it could not procure things desperately needed from the outside, and its industry had virtually collapsed. Moreover, it was in full civil and external war. The energies of the industrial population were almost entirely devoted to this war, and the peasantry did not respond to the fact of the war or to the meaning of the blockade by the *Entente*. In all these respects, again, Cuba's situation is quite different. Cuba may feel menaced by the United States, but she is in fact not at war. Nor is she under any effective economic blockade: she is actively trading with many countries, including those of the Soviet bloc.

Of course, there are many other reasons why revolutions have led to reigns of terror and to long dictatorships. But in the case of the early Soviet Union, those I have mentioned were certainly among the most important. In this connection, I should also like to underline the Cuban statement, in letter four, of the anti-Stalinist character of their general strategy of industrialization. That statement, I think, is a correct statement of the

[4] Bertrand Russell, *The Theory and Practice of Bolshevism* (London: George Allen & Unwin, 1920). For a detailed account see E. H. Carr, *A History of Soviet Russia* (London: Macmillan, 1950 and following, in several volumes).

facts so far and of the accepted plans now under way. Moreover, in fact and in plan, those in charge of the industrialization of Cuba are very much aware of what they are doing and what they do not want to do. Continued economic progress, of just the sort that *is* being made in Cuba today, is a major condition leading us to a hopeful view of the political outcome of the revolution in Cuba.

VII

What impresses me most of all about the cultural possibilities in Cuba are the eagerness to learn and the open-mindedness of many of the young men who make up the revolutionary Government of Cuba. In 20 years of teaching and writing, and of considerable travel, I have never before encountered such a sustained passion for learning, and such an intelligent awareness of the kinds of things that must be studied. And yet one of my major worries for Cuba is my worry for her cultural establishment. I do not mean only art and literature; I mean culture more broadly to include all those institutions of the mass media of communication and of higher and lower education by which the character and the mentality of men and women are formed.

The chief danger, I think, is quite simple: it is lack of qualified personnel. I mean this in two senses: first, in the ordinary sense of an absence of enough people with skill and knowledge and sensibility; but secondly, I am referring to this absence combined with the felt menace of counterrevolution and with the fact of a generally uneducated population. This combination *could* lead to the easy way out: the absolute control of all means of expression and the laying down of a Line to be followed.

Surely the more intelligent Cubans are correct, in their views expressed in letter seven, that at just this point above all others, the U.S.—as a Government or as a set of private individuals—could help mightily. The opportunity *is* there; in my view, it is not only an opportunity, it is a duty.

In their understandable euphoria about their educational accomplishments and plans, some Cubans, I think,

tend to exaggerate the speed with which a truly educated personnel can be developed. Education of the sort
needed in countries like Cuba, especially in the higher
schools of learning, cannot now be provided by Cuban
personnel. It is into *this* vacuum, and not into any military zone, that "extra-Hemispheric" forces are most
likely to move and most likely, in my judgment, to be
successful in their influences. The meaning of this fact
for the United States is again obvious.

Yet I rather doubt that it is at all obvious to the people in charge of such matters in the United States. What
intellectuals in Cuba are interested in, I doubt that the
U.S. Department of State, as presently constituted, is
capable of providing. For example, the interest of Cubans
in all varieties of Marxism, in all varieties of left-wing
thinking and politics, I find both understandable and ad-
mirable. For it is simply a fact that in practical and intellectual matters of the sort Cubans now confront, ideas
of this sort are relevant; it is also a fact that the kinds
of ideas officially acceptable in the United States, and ap-
proved by dominant sections of the U.S. intellectual
community, are largely irrelevant, indeed often meaningless, for Cuban educational, administrative and cultural
needs.

The North American public is generally ignorant of
the varieties of left-wing thought and activity. At the
same time it is true that some of the best and most schol-
arly studies of these subjects are now being carried on
in our leading universities. Yet the result of these studies do not get through to any larger public: they are
confined to "specialists." That simple fact, I believe, is
one reason why we cannot understand what the leaders
and the peoples of the hungry-nation bloc are thinking,
what they are trying to do, and what they are going to
be thinking and doing in the future.

In the U.S. newspapers, all of it is simply lumped together as "communism," and communism is treated as an
unchanging and homogeneous piece of evil.

The result for the citizen is plain ignorance about what
most of the world is up to. It is the ignorance of the created provincial—intellectually and politically. Accordingly, it is no wonder that when events occur which can-

not properly be understood, it leads to hysteria. The only insurance against such hysteria is knowledge—not the knowledge in one book or in a dozen books, but the knowledge that can only be provided by a genuinely free press whose management and whose journalists know what is important, know how to understand it and to explain it day by day and week by week. Such a press does not exist anywhere in the world.

That is one reason why the greatest thing for the cause of freedom any American foundation could do today would be to take up and to support, *in Cuban terms and under Cuban direction,* the idea expressed in letter seven of a genuinely international university in Havana. And to follow it up by arranging publication in the United States, as well as elsewhere, of the continuing results of such a promising intellectual and political effort.

VIII

So again, we come back to the same theme: As we think about what is happening in Cuba and about the argument of the Cuban revolutionary, as we try to speculate well about the probabilities of Cuba's future, we are forced again and again to reflect upon the actual and the possible part in these matters by the United States of America. We cannot avoid this. It is a major element of Cuba's problems—and of Latin America's. And it is a major element of our problems as citizens of the United States.

No one can make up his mind about something like the Cuban revolution, or about U.S.-Cuban relations, without answering questions of a much larger scope. Two such questions seem to me immediately relevant:

1: Is it possible today to have a society that is economically just and sensible and at the same time politically fluent and free? This is an old question, an ultimate question, a continuing question—and no one knows the answer to it. Despite the burden of the Cuban past, and the consequences of U.S. policies—past and present—I believe that Cuba does now represent a real chance for the development of one form of such a society. (There are, of course, many possible forms.)

2: Is it politically possible, economically viable, and militarily realistic for a country such as Cuba to achieve a thoroughly neutralist and genuinely independent orientation in world affairs? Despite the systematic myopia of U.S. policies towards Cuba, and the astuteness of Soviet policy, I believe there is still a chance. To increase that chance, I believe, is the only realistic goal the United States can now take up in her Cuban policy.

When we deal with history, we are not dealing in certainties; we are dealing with chances. But in the case of Cuba today, we are dealing with chances in the outcome of which we are ourselves deeply involved.

It is not easy at this moment for North Americans to listen well to what the Cuban revolutionaries are saying about the world in which they live. But it is just this that we must do. We must see behind their revolutionary rhetoric to their purposes and to their accomplishments. We must understand that if they are exaggerating North American iniquities, their exaggerations are surely well balanced by North American spokesmen in their assertions about Cuba. Perhaps a little reflection would reveal that neither country is in the altogether sad condition imagined by spokesmen of the other. Above all, we must not allow our reactions to the *manner* of the Cuban accusations to hide from us the fact that many of their complaints about the United States, past and present, are solidly based upon historical and sociological fact. We must not believe that the genteel mannerisms of U. S. spokesmen are an answer to these complaints; on the contrary, we must realize that this pose is a way of escaping the argument. We must address ourselves to the very real basis of Cuba's case; we must answer—with fact, with reason, and with civilized policies—the argument of these revolutionaries of the hungry-nation bloc.

NOTES AND ACKNOWLEDGMENTS

1.   It is very difficult to get hard facts from reliable documentary sources about Cuba. The old order was a tyranny; and tyrannies do not like readily available facts. It is equally difficult in the new Cuba: reliable means for the collection and authentication of facts are not as yet properly organized—and the facts, even fundamental facts, are changing very rapidly. Cuban agencies of information and Cuban personnel trained in techniques of documentary and statistical collection do not exist in any adequate way. Many hard facts, as well as competent estimates, do of course exist. But they are scattered about in many heads and files. One does not know which ministry has charge of which kinds of fact and document.

I wish therefore to thank Señora Margery Rios, Olga Finlay and Carlos Martinez for the diligent research work and the extraordinary efforts they have performed for me. The memoranda and statistical collections they gathered have been indispensable even when I have not been able to use them directly in this book.

2.   The best recent book on Latin America as a whole cf which I know is by Edward Lieuwen, *Arms and Politics in Latin America* (Council on Foreign Relations—New York; Praeger, 1960); see also J. J. Johnson, *Political Change in Latin America: The Emergence of the Middle Sectors* (Stanford University, 1958). See the excellent bibliographies given in these books. A careful, statistical survey of this world region by Otto Feinstein will be found in Volume I, Number One, of the magazine *New University Thought*. Also useful and convenient are two books by Lewis Hanke: *Mexico and the Caribbean* (New York: D. Van Nostrand Company, Inc.,

"Modern Latin America, Continent in Ferment," Vol. I, 1959); and *South America* (New York: D. Van Nostrand Company, Inc., "Modern Latin America, Continent in Ferment," Vol. II, 1959). On the Monroe Doctrine and related matters, see *Readings in American Foreign Policy,* edited by Robert A. Goldwin, with R. Lerner and C. Stourzh (New York: Oxford University Press, 1959).

In addition to these, I have used in "Note to the Reader, II" the excellent essay by Paul Johnson, "The Plundered Continent," *New Statesmen,* 17 September 1960; Edmundo Flores, "The Significance of Land-Use Changes in the Economic Development of Mexico," *Land Economics,* May 1959; Fredrick B. Pike and Donald W. Bray, "The Future of United States-Chilean Relations," *The Review of Politics* (University of Notre Dame, July 1960); Oscar Lewis, "Mexico Since Cárdenas," undated monograph (to appear shortly in *Investigacione Economica*); and A. A. Berle Jr., "The Cuban Crisis: Failure of American Foreign Policy," *Foreign Affairs,* October 1960. A useful tabulation of "American Investment in Cuba" has been made by Donald Villarejo, and appears in *New University Thought,* Vol. One, No. 1, Spring 1960.

3.   Books on the Cuban revolution are quickly outrun by events, but that does not mean that they are outdated. The most recent book—and the best—is by Leo Huberman and Paul Sweezy, *Cuba: The Anatomy of a Revolution* (New York: Monthly Review Press, 1960), which covers the revolution until about April 1960. On the insurrectionary phase of the revolution, Ray Brennen's *Castro, Cuba and Justice* (New York: Doubleday, 1959), and Jules Dubois, *Fidel Castro* (New York: Bobbs-Merrill, 1959), are informative. The fundamental work on the economy of the old order is: International Bank for Reconstruction and Development, *Report on Cuba* (Washington, D. C., 1950). Also indispensable: Lowry Nelson, *Rural Cuba* (Minneapolis: University of Minnesota Press, 1950); Leland H. Jenks, *Our Cuban Colony* (New York: Vanguard Press, 1928); U.S. Department of Commerce, *Investment in Cuba*

(Washington, D. C.: Government Printing Office, 1956);
Foreign Policy Association, *Problems of the New Cuba*
(New York: Foreign Policy Association, 1935).

4.   Of general historical accounts of U.S.-Cuban relations, I have found most useful: William Miller, *A New
History of the United States* (New York: George Bra-
ziller, Inc., 1958); Richard Hofstadter, William Miller
and Daniel Aaron, *The American Republic* (two volumes. Englewood Cliffs, N. J.: Prentice-Hall, Inc., 1959).
I have also drawn upon the files of the *New York
Times, Business Week, Foreign Affairs, Fair Play, The
Wall Street Journal, The Nation* (especially articles ap-
pearing here by Carleton Beals), and other periodicals
containing material on Cuba. My fundamental sources,
however, are my own interviews and observations in
Cuba.

liquidation of privledges, 61
the loss of a crooked dream, 61

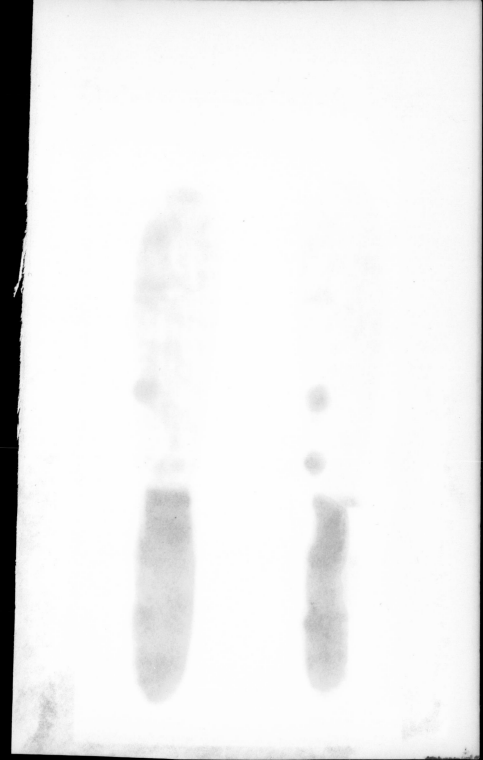

DATE DUE

OCT 2 5 2006	

GAYLORD   PRINTED IN U.S.A.